MEMOIRS OF A BROKEN QUEEN

AN ANTHOLOGY

S. Abdullah • Trina Baker • Honey Bee • Michelle Brannon • Monique Reed-Bumpers • Norma Gonzalez • Zynovia Hetherington • Carolyn Johnson • Elnah Jordan • Nahni Lynn • Anita Koyier-Mwamba • Aisha Newchurch • Natalia Pierson • Fonci Richardson • Salma Salah • Larnette Slade • Kimberly Suazo-Valentin • Linda Upshaw

Brown Girls Publishing
Seattle, WA

All rights reserved. No part of this publication may be reproduced, distributed or transmitted in any form or by any means, including photocopying, recording, or other electronic or mechanical methods, without the prior written permission of the publisher, except in the case of brief quotations embodied in critical reviews and certain other noncommercial uses permitted by copyright law. For permission requests, write to the publisher, addressed "Attention: Permissions Coordinator," at the address below.

Brown Girls Publishing
Seattle, Washington
www.browngirlswrite.org

Publisher's Note: This is a work of fiction. Names, characters, places, and incidents are a product of the author's imagination. Locales and public names are sometimes used for atmospheric purposes. Any resemblance to actual people, living or dead, or to businesses, companies, events, institutions, or locales is completely coincidental.

The writers contributing to *Memoirs of a Broken Queen: An anthology* retain copyrights on their individual works.

Memoirs of a Broken Queen: An anthology/ Edited by Christy Abram. -- 1st ed.
ISBN 9780615289342

This book is dedicated to beautiful brown girls far and wide, who bravely share their stories, love, and strength with the world. We love you. We need you. Thank you.

11-9-2019

To: Dr. Holland

Thank you very much for coming to the Book Signing

Take Care.

Always Love,

Lavell

This book contains subject matter about sexual assault and/or violence, and loss, which may be triggering to survivors.

Contents

1. **Soul Redemption**	*Monique Reed-Bumpers*	1
2. **It Comes from Somewhere**	*Honey Bee*	11
3. **Crushed**	*Zynovia Hetherington*	19
4. **How Dare He**	*Michelle Mitchell-Brannon*	35
5. **Motherhood**	*Carolyn Johnson*	41
6. **Bonded by Brokenness**	*Kim Suazo-Valentin*	53
7. **Monsters**	*Norma Gonzalez*	79
8. **Wealth and Sensibility**	*Anita Koyier-Mwamba*	85
9. **Dare to Be Free**	*Linda Upshaw*	93
10. **Eye of the Storm**	*Elnah Jordan*	105
11. **Three-Seventeen**	*Aisha Newchurch*	113
12. **Claiming My Magic**	*Natalia Pierson*	129
13. **Our Journey is One**	*Nahni Lynn*	135
14. **Collateral Lessons**	*Salma Salah*	145
15. **My Rose in Bloom**	*Fonci Richardson*	153
16. **Because I Love You**	*S. Abdullah*	169
17. **Lessons to Blessings**	*Larnette Slade*	173
18. **Survival of the Fittest**	*Trina Baker*	181
About the Authors		187

MONIQUE REED-BUMPERS

Soul Redemption

It was a scorching July day. I was Northbound on I-15 somewhere between Honeyville, Utah and Malad, Idaho. In a divided frame of mind; birthing the moment of reckoning in which my spiritual compass would be recalibrated. My destination was Seattle. In all actuality, the destination was the only item of certainty.

The only comfort found in this portion of my desolate journey was the back and forth chatter between my heart and head, accompanied by the burdening weight of brokenness. The music playing was drowned out by endless mind chatter; scattered thoughts and, soul cries, mingled with questions. Not only was I overwhelmed, but I was also emotionally bankrupt. "Life" had simply taken its toll, and nothing seemed manageable. Simply stated, there were too many things to fix, and I was ill-equipped to apply concentration to the issues that plagued my heart.

My vehicle was loaded fender to fender with every stitch of clothing and toiletry I possessed. More than luggage and totes stacked to the ceiling, I was suffocating under the weight of emotional baggage. I had a grip on nothing, my hands were too full. Full of a lot of shit that just wasn't mine to carry.

I had been fired from my job, a position in which I fought feverishly to prove my ability and worth. The loss had thrown my personal earth out of orbit, but there was more, so much more. I couldn't help but feel like a failure on every level. My body was plagued in suffering from Lupus, a horrendous autoimmune disease; also, a far too common diagnosis among women of color with absolutely no cure.

The disease itself is intensified and fueled by stress, which was the one thing I had a surplus of. Not only had I tainted the relationships with my two grown sons, Royce age twenty-five and Ra'Zhan age nineteen (my sun and my moon). My greatest fear was a seemingly harsh reality that these relationships were in a permanent state of disrepair. I walked around for five years with a gaping hole in my soul left by the murder of the only man I'd ever loved. Not just my love—my first love and soul tie who lived his latter thirty-two years in a cycle of addiction; the results of which wreaked havoc on our nineteen-year marriage.

"Bump" was my private education in how not to allow the 'issues of a man' to prevent me from loving him fully. With him is where I earned my stripes. As if this wasn't enough to wallow in, the crevices of my brokenness were filled with identity issues.

Being told I was adopted at age nine wasn't remotely as mind blowing as finding out I was half white (bi-racial) at age twenty. This, along with the separation of my parents, shortly after my high school graduation, left me feeling as though my entire life had been a lie. The unearthing of this secret created a rift of regret between my mother and me that birthed a spirit of heaviness. She was angry. I had retraced the steps of my adoption at age twenty-one. I had made her feel inadequate and disrespected. My question was left unanswered.

Less than three months after angering my mother by asking her why she hid the truth from me, she passed away unexpectedly, and she did so angry with me for my "need to know." There I was a tender twenty-one-year-old, semi-single mother of a two-year-old—due to my husband's incarceration in the

Utah State Penitentiary, and suddenly a motherless child. I felt I had no identity and no anchor, and I had begun to lean on cocaine as my constant companion, a battle that would be ongoing without expiration.

My present journey was the result of the immediate need to make a 'fight or flight' decision. While the flight was the appropriate decision; it was during the flight that I was forced to lean into many discomforts, seizing the only opportunity to reconcile my spirit, soul, purpose, and the redemption of my identity.

For the first time in my existence, I was less overwhelmed by the unknown and more fearful of everything familiar; especially with my 'old companion' within reach and without limit. This acknowledgement was the only confirmation that 'flight' was the correct decision.

For twenty-four years, I had relied upon everything that mother taught me. This journey was, however, bombarding me with everything that she had not. My intention is not to paint a picture of Doris Jean Reed being a bad mother, or not taking her role seriously. After all, my mother was barren as the result of a savage rape at eighteen. I was her chosen child, her hand selected angel whom she absolutely adored. Before I became a tom boy, I was her living doll.

My parents were affluent and successful, co-owners of the first black owned janitorial company in Utah during a period when life was particularly hard for people of color, especially in Utah. They provided an extraordinary life of privilege and more than enough of everything: private school education, formal piano lessons, ballet training, and endless travel.

My father, a hard worker and excellent provider, was often busy running from one jobsite to another. While my mother was my nurturer, teacher, and supreme disciplinarian.

There were times when the discipline scared me, but ultimately, it strengthened me. My parents were both vehemently strict and sheltering, stressing nothing as intensely as my education. Mommy was a sight to behold with her perfect chocolate complexion and petite frame. Always meticulous in her appearance, reserved, soft spoken exuding not only an educated demeanor but one of regal beauty, class, and a touch of sass.

Nothing about her existence demonstrated she was a country girl born and raised in Montrose, Arkansas, other than her cooking, which is my most valued tradition passed on through generations.

While she passed on every one of the elite qualities that she possessed in terms of being a graceful woman, a compassionate friend, loyal wife, and a woman of supreme character. She also passed on the vacancy of her inabilities. This is not to her discredit.

This is merely what I attribute many things such as; slave trauma passed on from my great-great grandmother – a living secret as the child of a slave and slave master. After all, she was the only child born to my grandmother and the 3rd generation of women who grew up in the darkness of Jim Crow. There was a stigma passed along to generations of women that struggled daily.

Black women faced harsh realities while living in constant fear of the established patterns of racism. They did not have the power of choice and certainly not an equal choice without punishment or persecution. These strifes were never supposed to rise to the surface or be discussed in decent company. Southern women were expected to be strong- not just strong but unbreakable, silent, and utterly self-sacrificing. Issues relative to emotions were not relevant to emotional processing, serving no greater purpose than to be submerged deep within oneself. She couldn't complain, speaking of her hurt and tears were a sign of weakness.

One of many misgivings was that children were to be seen and not heard. If there was something we didn't like, offended or wounded us, there was a silent expectation that we would "hush up" and hold our angst in the shadows of our heart. There was this unspoken rule even if you were grown, you never grew up to your mother, and some things would simply remain unspeakable, as addressing them would be construed as disrespect. Life was ordered. What you felt was irrelevant because everything was dictated to you, from clothing to behavior and feelings—you simply felt what you were told to feel, and the rest was left unaddressed.

There was no counseling for the generations of sexual abuse or physical abuse and "whoopings," which were impartations of the slave master to inflict fear and used as a means of control. There was certainly no thought or premise of self-acceptance nor practices of affirming self-love, self-care was nonexistent.

I watched what seemed to be a routine and commonly passive response to adulterous husbands which was to "turn a blind eye," and "let that man be a man," simply because he was the provider. Even though he was distorting the proper view of the family image. It was almost as if they were given passes of permission if the home front was stable and secure.

I observed women in my family be complacently submissive and at times subservient to their men. That is not to say there was not love beneath the surface. It is to say that tolerance of certain things was confusing and misguiding. These examples I spent my life observing are what kept me holding on to a turbulent marriage that was rooted in the foundation of love and friendship yet, toxic from the victimization of addiction.

That is only one of many examples of the lies women of our culture have somehow allowed themselves to live. Women of color have become so engulfed by their roles as wives, mothers, daughters, employees, and other roles that have expectations that identities are lost.

Lost in the abyss of trying to reach the status quo, lost in the darkness of the shadows of the expectations of us set by others. Lost in in the brow beating of what others categorized for us as failures. These circumstances have led to overwhelming experiences when arriving at various milestones in life.

The milestones that we encounter in our journey are unpredictable and wide ranging. We may find ourselves with our nests empty, arriving at retirement, standing in the rubble of dissolved relationships, divorce or dealing with the demise of a loved one.

While the milestone is unpredictable, the certainty is we find ourselves with our hands full. Full of everything people who have touched our lives have left behind; along with a stench and residue of what was passed onto us. We lack the knowledge of how to correctly cleanse our spirits and purge ourselves from repeating the ancestor's errors.

I have not only arrived but have adapted to my destination. I have begun to settle in a new space as my personal sanctuary. In doing so, I am also unpacking my baggage and releasing the boulders that have left me emotionally scarred and sutured my wounds.

It is with respect and admiration for my mother Jean, my Big Mama (grandmother) Labertha, great-grandmother Estella, and finally my Mambo great-great grandmother Maw-Maw, that I will break these toxic traits of overlooking self for the sake of others. It is in memory and celebration of my ancestors that I will do what they were not allowed to and break the shackles of bound emotions. It is for my future generations that I will backtrack with my sons and embark on a journey of emotional healing to become the safe place I should have been for them from day one.

My greatest faults and flaws as a parent were my belief that my job was to provide food, clothing, shelter, and dictate the lives they would live. I will instead plant and plow a garden so my seed holders may flourish without flaws inflicted upon them.

I will intentionally teach them all I learn in this new season of self-reflection, sharing with them the implementation of boundaries and making self-love the ultimate priority. I will propel forward with the energy and the light of the ancestors who not only produced but nourished me in their abilities. Never to reside in the darkness of secrecy, silence, and shame again.

HONEY BEE

It Comes from Somewhere

Something was wrong, I could feel it even before I saw my father's black dodge stratus in my elementary school roundabout. The wind tickled my skin through my jacket and my stomach churned, despite the absence of hunger. With the sight of his car came a wave of confusion, then worry—then fear; this is not right...it was not his day. *Where was my mother?*

My father is a lovable but awkward man; when he is nervous, he jumps from subject to subject in a circle of an ever-expanding topic he is trying to avoid. In this case, the topic was my mother. When I got in the car, he talked about everything but her, hurling fast sentences at me about nothing at all. His avoidance encouraged fear to plant roots in my body, spreading worry faster than I could control. When we arrived at our favorite music shop, and he took me inside. I demanded to know what was going on with my mother.

The response came after half an hour of idling inside the music store, during which I relentlessly showered him with questions. "Is mom, ok? Why did you pick me up? Where is my sister? Why aren't you speaking to me?" Every inquiry was answered with, "I'll tell you when we are outside." Once outside, we got halfway to the car before I asked a final time: "Dad, what's going on!" He continued walking, then stopped at the driver door and put his hand on the car with tears pooled in his eyes, "Something has happened with your mom and Martin."

Before I knew it, one thought clouded the rest, taking over my mind and body and locking me in a freeze: *He killed her.* Devastation, pain, and sadness flooded me all at once, and I collapsed into the car, knowing my world had just changed. My father tried talking to me, but I was trapped in my head, reviewing my life, and the few years I could remember. Feelings for my mother came in waves, but one thing I notice when I look back was the lack of surprise. I was not shocked.

There is a before and an after to this story, as with all stories of its kind. The after is that my mother was not actually dead. Her then-boyfriend (now husband) and she had a physical altercation that landed her in jail overnight, hence why she couldn't pick me up from school. She was released from jail later that day; a large gauze bandage was placed on the spot where her boyfriend's head made contact with hers. Her hair was disheveled, and the skin around her eyes was inflamed from prolonged crying. We reunited in tears and whispered promises to never let anything like that happen again.

The before is abuse: emotional abuse, physical abuse, and dysfunction. Bruises and scrapes not large enough to warrant interference but consistent enough to know what was happening.

Arguments, screaming matches, and throwing things. After the incident was much the same, if not watered down; the distance was between them now, but still the marks appeared, the words still yelled, and tears continued to fall.

As time went on, they hid it better. They moved in together, got dogs, and worked from home. The abuse became more emotional and by now a staple in their relationship. It was the tragic foundation of who they were together, the invisible iceberg under the seemingly harmless chunk of ice that was their relationship.

This is not the worst thing to have ever happened to my nine-year-old self, nor is it the best. My mind created a narrative to normalize the dysfunction of my childhood, and I carried that message with me throughout adolescence and into adulthood, always reminding myself that no matter how bad I had it, people had it worse. Children are abused. Families go through traumatic extremes to provide for their children. Parents actually die, all those are worse than what I had to go through.

As I grew up and moved out, I soon had relationships with men, that on a smaller scale, resembled the relationships I had grown accustomed to. I would put their needs before my own, shrinking myself to accommodate their undisturbed presence in my life. I thought sacrifice translated as love. I told myself, *put others before yourself, and let them do what they want with you*. It was selflessness, loyalty, care. In my mind, my pain mattered less than their happiness and satisfaction.

It took many unhealthy relationships to recognize what I had learned and internalized from childhood was not my truth. I did not want to be treated as an object but like a person. I wanted to feel respected instead of minimized. I realized that when I showed up in these relationships, I had shown up as a woman who had not been taught to value herself. I understood that I had internalized the message that I was less important.

Through my mother's relationships, I was taught to place my worth in the hands of men instead of recognizing and demanding my own worth. These lessons ultimately led me to minimize my experiences and foster a deep sense of shame each time I felt pain. With that revelation came sadness and anger, but it also came with a sense of clarity. I now knew who and what I wanted to be. I wanted to feel like I was enough. I wanted to show up in relationships secure in my own identity; all that remained was the task of letting go and allowing myself to grow. Once I realized this, things began to fall in place, things that were previously clouded by the wall of shame I had built around my trauma and myself.

I grasped the fact that I was raised in a highly dysfunctional household where emotional abuse was common. The reason I did not feel any shock that day with my mother was that the abuse was normal. In my nine-year-old mind, my mother being killed by her boyfriend was an idea that, while still triggering, did not surprise me. I had already learned and normalized the idea that men hurt women; it was a part of my life, something that held significant space in my reality.

These ideas and lessons that exist to harm and keep us in a state of emotional toxicity are present in every facet of life. We are taught what is acceptable, scolded for what is tolerable, and shamed for what is disagreeable—without ever having a say in what standard we are held to. We are discouraged from questioning our circumstances, exploring ourselves, and feeling our feelings; fearful of what we might find.

This is all to say one thing: we do not choose what we are taught. During my formative years, I did not choose to internalize, normalize, and expect abuse; it was a coping mechanism. I did not consciously choose to believe messages that media and society pushed about black women, I was simply not presented with any other option. For protection, I built a wall around my feelings as a survival technique from the emotional turmoil of my childhood. I was taught all of these things that I now realize I do not believe and accept but that because I was raised with them and told not to question them.

This is all to say one thing: you cannot escape your trauma. It will be there, even when you feel that you have left it behind. Even when you have buried it so deep that you can hardly remember, it will find its way back to you—slowly creeping into your life at inopportune moments. It will fight you for however long you fight it.

The advice I want to offer is, you don't have to escape your trauma. Healing it, not fighting it, will allow the peace you deserve. To heal, you must accept that pain, embrace it. Allow it the life it was so deeply denied. Let yourself feel everything you were told you didn't deserve to feel. You will discover that your trauma is not trying to overtake you; it simply wants to be put to rest.

This process is one that takes a lifetime and then some. Trauma can weave itself deeply into our minds, our bodies, our generations. It will not be resolved in one day. But we can work each day to acknowledge it, allow it to complete its cycle, and continue with a little more room for joy in our lives.

ZYNOVIA HETHERINGTON

Crushed

I was so tired of coming down to the Detroit Greyhound bus station, it smelled of pee, and somebody was always asking me for change. "I ain't got no change," I replied, doing my best to avoid the stench of urine and alcohol. I used to be so mad cause mama wouldn't let her boyfriend take me downtown. I could hear her from the bedroom with booze in her voice, "She can catch the bus, it won't kill her." My mother's boyfriend, Uncle Jim, is the best man I had ever known. Except for my father's brother, Uncle

Carl who lived down south. They always treated me so nice and never-ever even tried to touch me or say anything inappropriate to me; as so many men in my life had done. They treated me like they were my father and uncle and nothing else. Sometimes I'd pray that when I woke up, one of them would be my daddy.

The bus station was so big, it extended a whole block. Nestled in the center of downtown Detroit, it was a haven for homeless people and transients with nowhere to go. That Saturday, I was on a mission to see my sister at work. She worked as a manager at Burger King. She looked so beautiful and professional in her uniform. The Burger King was attached to the bus station but seemed like a whole different world when I went inside.

It was clean and smelled good, like bleach and Pine-Sol, two of my favorite spells. The bathrooms were clean, and they had a security guard that kept people from hanging around. I came down a few days a week to pick up my nephew, Jules. Jules and I are less than seven years apart, we were more like brother and sister. My sister was a single parent, so I did all I could to help her. I didn't mind. Her home was safe, a far cry from my home life.

Sometimes I had a bad attitude because it might be snowing, cold or raining, and the buses were full of creepy men that would always make comments about my body. I never knew if they might try something. Sometimes men would try to touch me, especially if it was dark.

 I really loved taking care of my nephew, he thought I was so much older and listened to me. When I would get to the restaurant to pick him up, I always got to have whatever I wanted from the menu. Sometimes, my sister would surprise us with money for the movies. We mostly went to the Palms Theatre because they had the double feature karate movies. I never told my sister that sometimes we'd see a scary movie, it was our little secret.

♛

In 1979, I was twelve years old, waiting to turn thirteen. Turning thirteen marked the beginning of being a "real teenager." I had no idea what that meant. I heard people talking about becoming a teenager, so I anticipated better times. I had noticed over the last year, my body changing, rounding in my hips, my chest grew buds that were sore if I bumped them. The worst was when the stupid boys in my class would try to squeeze my butt or my chest. I would scratch them with my nails that were long and unkept, so the edges were ragged, sometimes drawing blood. Although in my eyes, it was self-defense and they got what they deserved, I would get suspended for three days; which secured lots of cussing, yelling, and a whooping with a few switches.

That summer, I would go to Burger King and sometimes stay all day with my nephew instead of going to my sister's house. Many of the employees would come and sit with us during their breaks and lunch. Two of my sister's employees were also her close friends. They would come to her house, and sometimes they would all go out together, and I would babysit my nephew. Both friends were males in their early twenties. I felt comfortable around them because they were like my big brothers, I felt this way because of their relationship with my sister.

At the end of the summer, one of the young men, Barry, began to pay attention to me in a different way. He was very handsome, milk chocolate skin color, only a few feet taller than me at 5'3", he had a very short hair-cut with brush waves. Barry always dressed casually, with jeans and a polo shirt, he had a nice short mustache, and he smelled like old spice cologne, a scent I was familiar and comfortable with. He would give me compliments and ask me for hugs. He asked me about going back to school and if I had a boyfriend. I noticed that he only talked to me like this when we were alone. I often sat on my sister's porch, and when they would come over, he would linger behind or come back outside and talk to me.

That's when it began, my "crush." I felt special when Barry talked to me. I found myself waiting for his next visit and thinking about him when I was at home. Barry made me feel pretty. He always noticed my outfits and my hair, giving me compliments, which I had not received from others in my life. Most of the time I felt very ugly and un-special in anyway.

♛

One fall, I was surprised to see Barry coming up the block because my sister was not home yet. I was happy. It had been a few weeks, and I was missing his attention. My crush had grown without contact with him because I made up things in my mind that he would say to me and how I would respond.

He came up on the steps and immediately asked for a hug. I happily gave him one, and I felt his hand rub my butt. I recall looking around because I knew he was crossing a line. His embrace felt different. Different than talking and very different from my imagination. He sat down and started asking me questions about school, lunch, and finally, did I have a boyfriend that was "taking his girl."

I gushed, and repeated the question "taking your girl?" He paused, then looked into my eyes, "Yes, you know you my girl, right? A quiet "yes" was all I could mutter, it was enough; the next question was, "Well, can you teach me how to kiss?" I knew this was not a real question, but I also knew what he was asking for, again a quiet "yes" was all I managed to say. The kiss started out as I expected, closed mouth and just lips touching, and then it became a grown-up kiss when he thrust his tongue in my mouth. I did not know how to respond, so I pulled back, he held my head and turn it sideways, to control me.

It felt like forever, but I know it lasted a couple of seconds. My eyes filled with tears, but Barry did not respond. He jumped up and off the porch and warned me not to tell my sister he came by. I sat on the steps, stunned and not knowing how to feel. To make sense of the situation, I thought, *I am his girl, and that's what girlfriends do, right?* A part of me wanted to tell, but I knew there was no one I could tell. No one listened all the other times I told, and a kiss was the least of things I had experienced starting at the age of three. That's when my older cousin started molesting me.

The fall seemed to blow by, and as usual in Detroit, the winter roared in with snow and freezing cold. I was still looking forward to my December birthday. My sister had started giving me a little money for keeping my nephew, so I thought that connected to me turning thirteen. I was always happy to hang with my nephew, who was getting older and more of a companion. We laughed together, told little jokes, and watched TV.

One night in November, one month before my birthday, my sister asked if I would babysit because she and the Burger King gang were going out. It had been months since she had gone out and I was happy to see her dressed up and out of her Burger King uniform: blue pants, light blue shirt, bow tie, and keys—lots of keys. I said yes and was also thinking about the little change I would be getting because I was hoping to buy a pair of jeans from Kmart for my birthday.

That Saturday night, it was cold, and there was already snow on the ground from the first or second snowstorm. I never really kept count because the Detroit public school would never close unless it was a record-breaking snowstorm, I never knew the record until it was broken.

By this time, I literally lived three blocks over from my sister, thanks to Uncle Jim. He worked at a large car factory and moved us into a nice house, the best place we ever lived. My sister lived in a four family flat a few blocks over, and I was overjoyed to have her so close. The only problem was that she had stabilized her schedule and my nephew was in school full day. I did not have to babysit as much, and therefore, my safe haven was limited. I was not allowed to just go and visit or just stay at her house, no explanation was given, mom just said "no."

So, like clockwork, my sister's night out was planned. I walked over to her house all bundled up to block the below freezing windchill. Upon arrival, my sister and two other females were present. Then Michael, Barry's homeboy came, and I was surprised and a little disappointed to see him alone. They all left shortly after he arrived then I began to prepare my nephew for bed. It was around 9:30pm. He fell asleep in his mom's bed, watching TV, which of course was against my sister's rules. I went back into the living-room and turned on the big TV in hopes of finding one of my favorites on, like Shirley Temple or Godzilla. The knock on the door scared me. I started looking around the room for what I do not know, but I walked slowly to the door and looked out the curtain like my mom used to when the people would come to shut off the water.

There he was, Barry; stomping his feet as many people do while at your door in the winter. Shaking the snow off and preparing them self for the heat inside. I opened the door and said, "They gone"; without a pause, he said, "I know." My heart started beating fast at that very moment. Everything seemed to go in slow motion then lightning speed.

The question, this time without the teach-me caveat was, "Can I have a kiss?" Again, I muttered, "yes." His kiss did not start off soft, it was straight to "grown-up" style. Hard pressing on my pre-teen lips, thrusting his tongue, and me not sure what to do with my own. Not that he was my first kiss, not even my first "grown-up" kiss, but my first kiss, well second with a grown-up.

I was shifted off my feet to the floor, my pants and panties were pulled down at the same time, and Barry managed to get in between my legs and used my pants to lock me down. I remember the tears and the whispers of "no, no!" because screams which were what I was feeling, would have awakened my nephew and I could not risk that. I can still feel that horrible sting sometimes, though not nearly as often. The sensation between my legs burned. I had no control over my soon-to-be teenage body. My strength seemed non-existent. That face scratching 7th grader was powerless, no self-defense. The sound of his breath lingered in my ear for months, the musty smell as if he had been playing hours of basketball stung my nose, especially when I was in the gym at school. Finally, he got up, somewhat tangled in between my pants, I heard the door shut, and I laid there for I don't know how long, crying, stinging, burning, and powerless.

Months went by, I tried so hard to forget, and he stopped coming around. No one spoke of him. The word was he and his wife were having problems, so he was staying home. That was me ease dropping on "grown-folks talkin," as my mama would say. I never asked about him, my crush had been "crushed," and all the real and fantasized feelings and experiences were now covered with pain and fear. These feelings I knew well and were used to. Therefore, I was somewhat comforted by what I knew. That is until my 4th oldest sister asked me the question. "Hey, when was your last period?"

My sister, the oldest of the three of us, was the keeper of things, including hygiene items. She kept the pads and gave them to me when I requested. She gave me Tylenol when I was rolling around the floor with killer cramps and soon, I realized she kept a calendar of all three of our periods.

I answered honestly, "I don't know." I didn't, I had not even noticed that my cycle had not come, and I did not miss it. She began to ask me questions that I squirmed under. She then said, "I'm gonna tell mama to take you to the doctor." All I could say was, "For what?" Of course, I knew for what, but it just had never crossed my mind. So many other things were mixed up in my head. There was no space for *What if I am pregnant?*

I was off to the clinic a few days later. "Pee in this cup," the nurse requested. "The test is positive. You might want to get her sterilized, she probably gonna do it again!" This from the white doctor in the white coat that became a blur behind my tears. Out I ran to the bathroom, but it was through a lobby full of people, and I could not keep my sobs down. I came out, and there was an African American woman, name tag a blur, title, Social Worker.

She asked me questions that I would not answer. I kept my head down, careful not to look her in the face, thinking she would somehow know, or I would blurt out the truth. She told me the mostly correct answers. We determined that I was not a hoe and that someone had "done something to me." I would not say who, mainly because I had already decided that it was my fault. I had a crush on him, I flirted with him, I teased him, for goodness sakes, I kissed him. *Yes, it's true*, I thought, it was my fault I *got what I deserved just like with my older cousin and family friends*.

Decisions were made while I was in the bathroom and talking to the Social Worker. About a week later I was awakened at 6:00am, I remember because I had insomnia and always watched the clock my sister put in the hall. My sleeping area did not have a door, so I could look right out into the hall. Also, the light was kept on because we had rats, and this way, you could see if they were coming into your room. The plan was if you see or hear one just start making noise and they would run the other way, it worked most of the time.

Barely awake, I put on my school clothes which my sister was also responsible for making sure I had out the night before. This was not at my mama's direction, but her own plan because she hated being late for school and took it upon herself to make sure the three of us were up and out the house on time. I knew not to ask questions because I could smell the alcohol on my mama's breath and did not want to get a drunken yell. I got in the car and fell back to sleep.

I was awakened by the speed bumps going down into a parking garage, which I later realized was to a hospital. I walked to a waiting room with my mama.

After a while, we went into a small office where a nurse told us about the procedure. She explained that because I was past twenty weeks, I could not have an abortion, but would have to have the baby. There would be a solution shot into my stomach with a needle which would kill the baby within twenty-four hours, then I would deliver the still born child, and go home.

I heard every word, but it didn't fit into my already full mind, so I was alarmed and shocked at every step. Into a ward with seven other women, eight of us total, four on one side at four across the room. I don't recall making eye contact with anyone. I do remember that each of them delivered their already dead baby and left in about two days. I was the only one left, eight down to one.

The process took four days. The nurse gave me a shot in my IV to make me go into labor because a dead baby cannot push itself out. Many years later, when I had my daughter, I had to get the same shot to induce labor. I began to think about the feeling of having to push; this time, I took home a beautiful baby girl.

The nurses were nice. One nurse came and sat with me when the real labor hit. I felt pain my thirteen-year-old body couldn't explain. The nurse told me what I needed to do. She helped me get on the port-a-potty where the dead baby would go. The nurse instructed me not to look, "Just hit the call-button, "she said. "A nurse will come and get it."

"It" that's what she said, it stung for some reason, but I was still glad she was with me. On the afternoon of day four it happened, I delivered my already dead baby, I looked, I started screaming, they came and then I was asleep. Many years later, when I had my son, and he was stillborn, again, I screamed and looked at him, but this time, the nurse encouraged me to look at him and to say goodbye. I gained closure from his departure; his life was validated—not like at thirteen when I felt I didn't matter.

I woke up to the sensation of my mama shaking my shoulder, as I did four days prior. I got dressed in the same clothes, got in the same car, and went back to the same room. "Go lay down," my mama said, and I did. No one talked to me, no one asked any questions, no one cared.

A few weeks later, I was back to my life as it was, but it wasn't as it was, although it appeared that only I knew that. My second oldest sister was over, and I could hear her voice downstairs. It was clear that she was on the phone. I can't even say why I did it, but I picked up the phone in my sister's room, the keeper of things. I heard them talking. I could not make out all the female voices, but I heard, "With her fast ass. She out doing who knows what!"

"Girl, I know, just fast, too hot for her own good!"

So many statements, names, I still held the phone but couldn't seem to hear anymore. I then heard the dial tone. They knew something, they thought something, but it was wrong, wasn't it, or was it? I mean I had a crush on him, I flirted with him, I was a tease, I kissed him, and then I was "crushed."

Time passed as it always does, my external powerlessness continued until I was sixteen years old, which was the last time I was sexually abused. Unfortunately, I continued the cycle of self-abuse perpetuating that my abuser's indiscretions were my fault. I masked behaviors of self-hatred and low self-worth, with good grades, and hard work. I joined the Varsity Cheer squad, fought when necessary, then fell in love for real this time. He loved me back even after he heard all my secrets, well almost all them.

I met my knight in shining armor, a boy I had known since 6th grade. He had grown into a handsome young man. He stood 6'4 to my 5'4 stature, short haircut, mustache, very muscular from playing football, and a personality of compassion, love, and protection. I called him Choo, and after learning about the abuse I was experiencing from my brother-in-law and my sister's boyfriend, he confronted them with a threat to gather some gang members from his neighborhood to "deal" with them. That day was the last time either man touched me.

After the formal abuse ended, my life was in no way problem free, but I give my survival and victory through that journey to God. I began to pray again; I had stopped at thirteen. I wrote poems and talk to my school counselor about leaving Detroit. I was not healed, I was scabbed over, but it was enough to keep me going at least until it was ripped off by a different trauma. I have learned that scabs are only helpful if they're in the process of healing. Scabs cannot replace true healing. Healing takes time, pain, tears, and prayers, and help from those who are willing to go through the process with you.

Healing is not an experience that is done alone, if "It takes a village to raise a child," you better believe it takes one to heal one. I have a village now; an extended healing family. I have a physical and spiritual healing village.

I believe that true healing can take a lifetime, especially for those of us whose wounds started so very early. The process of healing is filled with struggle, pain, joy, strength, and love. I am on that path being supported and cheered on by my village members new and old. If I had to say one thing about my experience, it would be victory is mine, no longer am I powerless.

MICHELLE MITCHELL-BRANNON

How dare He

I was held captive and raped in a stall in a public bathroom. *How did this happen to me?* I was so confused. *Why is no one here to help me? Why me?* Thoughts rushed my mind as the pain from his grip surged through my body. The day started normal. I woke up and went to see if my friend Stephanie was home from her dad's house. Stephanie lived next door to my godmother, where I spent the last two summers. I knocked and was greeted by her brother Tony. He was tall, lanky, and nonchalant. "Steph is in her room," he pointed the way. I entered her room with a thrust, and there she was sitting on her bed with a big smile on her face.

"Hey, girl, I was hoping you would come over. I tried calling, but your phone line was busy," she said combing through her silky tresses.

"I'm here, now, what's up?" I found refuge on her bed.

"Girl I met this guy, and I want to tell you all about him," her face lit up. "He's 6 feet tall with smooth buttery caramel skin and a body that smells like heaven."

The more she talked, I could visualize him. I could see his "fineness" and smell him as the words fell from her mouth. Stephanie didn't always have the best taste in guys. The last guy she dated looked like a character from the movie *Space Jam*. Stephanie spent hours talking about how they met and how she had to sneak to meet him a few blocks away.

We lived in the heart of Seattle, and Marion street was where kids hung out. Stephanie made plans to meet them and did her best to persuade me to go. She knew her mom didn't mind her being there because it was close by. The more she talked, the more she smiled, "I can't wait to kiss him, she shared." I wished he was there to kiss her too so she would shut the hell up!

The doorbell rings and its Monica, Stephanie's friend, who I met this summer.

"Hey, ya'll ready to go?"

"Go, where?" I asked. They both laughed. Little did I know; they had planned a date with Stephanie's guy and a friend.

"What's funny?" I quizzed.

"Nothing!" Monica blurts out.

"We need you to come with us to the beach while we meet our friends," Stephanie says. I told my mom I was hanging out with you."

Why in the hell would I go? I thought. I don't feel like this shit, but I will never hear the end of it.

Monica and I hung at the park, while the couples were hugged up in the corner. I headed to the bathroom. As I walked in, I noticed a broken tile on the wall and floor. It smelled like the lake and felt cold and eerie. I looked towards the ceiling and noticed running water dripping down the side of the wall.

I moved to the side of the stall to avoid the dripping water. I opened the heavy silver metal stall then closed it and proceed to pee. Suddenly the door slams open and Monica's guy is pushing his way into the stall.

"What are you doing?" I belted. He preceded. "What are you doing!" I ask again this time a little louder. He looked and didn't say a word. His silence was piercing and far louder than the words. He had this empty look in his eyes and acted as if he didn't hear a word that fell from my shuttering lips.

I was terrified and riddled with fear—my heart raced as he was backing me up against the cold, dirty wall. I tried to scream, but nothing came out. I desperately wanted someone to hear my pain. I started to think about how I got there—*why did I come? How did I get myself in this position?* My mind raced, and I prayed it was a dream.

As I felt his hands wrap around my neck, I closed my eyes as tight as I could. I was afraid to look at him. He staggered close to kiss me. I turned my face to avoid his lips, but he strongly pressed his against mine. I instantly felt sick, his breath smelled of whiskey and cigarettes.

I saw him drinking and smoking with Monica earlier. He whispered, "If you scream, I will snap your neck. I'll kill you and your friends." He squeezed harder, "Bitch, did you hear me? I said I'll kill you first, then your friends." I nodded, he grabbed and turned my face towards him. The tears that once trickled where like broken levees overflowing a dam.

My body was overflowing with emotions as he pulled up my skirt and ripped off my panties. *One..two..three, one..two..three.* I tried to count in my head to distract myself from what was happening. I couldn't get past the number three. I thought, *what comes after three? Oh, God, please help me..one…two..three.* The sequence of the numbers continued to escape me. The numbers played through my mind like a skipping record.

I hoped someone; anyone would come to my rescue. I closed my eyes; I couldn't bear to see his face as he penetrated me. His touch made me sick to my stomach. Every groan, movement, and motion crippled me. "I can't breathe, I can't breathe, I uttered." He continued without pause. Pain riddled my body and settled in my chest. The pain I felt was unlike any pain I've ever felt. It cut deeper than any knife ever could. He broke me so deeply. I wasn't just broken; I was shattered, and I didn't have anyone to help me pick up the pieces. I knew from that moment I would never be the same.

Finally, he finished, although it lasted a few moments, it seemed like an eternity. He backed out of the stall has if I was no longer visible. I felt a sense of relief, but I was numb. I tried to pull myself together, but I collapsed. As he left, I heard him say, "Remember what I said." He closed the door behind him and disappeared.

I walked out of the bathroom, but I didn't see my friends. I felt relieved; I didn't want to pretend like I was ok. Instead, I ran down Lake Washington Boulevard as fast as I could. Lake Washington Boulevard was usually a happy place where families walked their dogs and admired the beautiful waterfront. I struggled to run, I felt heavy and tender, most importantly, I was afraid. Next anger came over me, *how dare he damage me even more.* I ran and ran until I made it back to my godmother's house.

As I went inside, my godmother asked was I hungry. "No, thanks, momma. I'm not hungry." I made a beeline to the bathroom, I needed to wash his stench from my body. I made the water so hot it nearly burned my skin. I scrubbed and scrubbed until my skin welted. I laid there, watching the tears dance down my cheek and meet the water as if they were entangled in an intimate embrace. I knew that day, my life was forever changed. I could not go back to the innocence I once knew.

I wish I could have stayed behind and remained the kid I deserved to be. I wish I would have just trusted myself to say no, but I was afraid to disappoint my friend. I wish I could have just said no, but I couldn't because I needed to belong. I wish I had my mom or dad to tell me I was enough and would always be enough so I wouldn't have ended the day in a more broken place.

CAROLYN JOHNSON

Motherhood

Wow, a baby having a baby. That is what I was, a baby having a baby. And even more than that, I was a troubled baby, having a baby, running from my problems. I was a young girl from the country where I loved to run free in the woods, up and down the trails. I was a girl that loved freedom, being free to run free, free to laugh and explore. Free to smell the beauty of the earth. Free to ponder why the clouds in the sky are just like they are and what it would be like to sit up there on top of them. How did they get so white and beautiful?

As a young girl, I loved running down through my family's horse pasture, hitting a section of scotch brooms. They were beautiful, deep forest green bushes with bright yellow blooming flowers. As I ran down the hill, they got taller and taller, urging me to run faster. Their scent was strong, filling the air with beautiful citrus perfume.

I followed the path through the middle of our pasture, as it opened to a huge field, where we kept our horses, played hide and seek, and held our secret camps where we hung out. Holding memories, good and bad, this pasture was the place we shared with special friends, staying there late in the night, looking at the stars, talking of our hopes and dreams, of what we wanted to become and where we would go. Being raised in Kirkland, Washington, all my friends were white, and most of them had very different stories than I did, but we loved hanging out together.

My world consisted of feeding the rabbits, collecting chicken eggs, and helping my mother till her garden. At the time, my friends and I did not care about color or race but were more concerned with having fun and running free. This pasture was a secret place for my friends and me, bringing a sense of freedom to us all. I can hear my mother's voice now, "Carolyn, it's time to come in. Send your friends home." That would be the first request, but we did not respond;

we were always trying to get the last laugh in or plan what we were going to do the next day. Before I knew it, I could hear my mother again, "If you don't get yourself home, I am going to come down there and beat you all the way home." My mother never beat us, but she made serious threats.

This same pasture and woods became my older brother's part time home. He was often at odds with my mother and father and instead of taking the whoopings, he would just stay outside in the pasture and hide, in hopes my father would just let whatever offence simply pass. I remember my mother telling us, "Go look for your brother and take him some food." No one ever wanted to go look for him; we would stand at the top of the hill and scream his name, receiving no response.

I always wanted my mom to fix my brother's situation by helping him to talk with my father, but my mother was not a good communicator. She rarely gave us instructions; it seemed she wanted us to figure everything out for ourselves. I needed more. I wanted my mother to talk to me more often, as well as my brother. But she was quiet, though she always did what she could to help us. As a teenager, I would regularly get upset with my mother without really knowing why. She was a quite strong lady. An extremely practical woman, she believed in saving. Our frugal mother was always trying to help my father by being self-sufficient, never needing much. One of fourteen children, she was the one in her family that had the same number of children as her mother. Mom birth five boys and nine girls. We were stair steps apart, born of the same father, same mother.

I can clearly remember, not feeling connected to my mother; I spent my adolescence always upset with her. I was also distant from my brothers and sisters, it seemed as though we never had anything to say to one another. I was the fifth oldest child and the fourth oldest daughter. My place in the family seemed to disappear as so often happens with middle children. Later, as we all got just a little bit older, we would tell stories and laugh and joke with one another. Sometimes we remembered the hard things. I heard the story concerning the death of my third oldest sister, Shirley Ann, who would have been two years older than me.

The story was told a couple of different ways, and through it, I started to understand my mother a little bit more with telling. I was told that Shirley Ann was a beautiful baby, a head full of stunningly black hair, very light in complexion like my mother. And in every telling, there seemed to be something unusual about her personality that made everyone think she was quite a special baby.

One night, tragedy fell on the family. Shirley Ann was crying relentlessly. Different family members tried to make her stop crying by giving her things to eat. She was given a piece of candy or a cough drop, then she was given a piece of a hot dog. When she began to choke, my sisters said our parents went into a panic mode, unable to dislodge whatever was blocking her breathing. While rushing her to the hospital, Shirley Ann died in my mother's arms.

When I heard this story from my sisters and my brother, I could see they were trying to explain that although our parents loved us all, their grief over the loss of this baby girl, who was only two years old, was a tragedy they never recovered from. Hearing this story helped me feel closer to my mother; it made me want to speak words of comfort to her, but I didn't know how.

My mother did her best; she fed us well; she kept us together. She stressed the importance of school. But my mother was not a talker, and she was not a nurturer. There were not many close hugs and kisses, and for me, not enough talking and teaching. I looked at my mother at times and saw how tired she was, how she was making the best out of what she had.

She was a beautiful lady, but I never saw my father hug her. And while I don't remember hearing them talking with each other, every nine to twelve months, mom would be with child, until she had fourteen. And the more they came, the more I felt lost, no direction, no help. I believe some of the other siblings felt the same, but I wasn't sure. The three above me stuck together, and the ones under me seemed to form another group. And that left me alone.

My second oldest sister was not living with us, but she would come home to visit and bring new and interesting things. At the time she and one of my brothers were into drugs—speed, acid, and Quaaludes. I remember my first encounter with speed; my brother gave it to me. It made me feel energetic and excited; this was so different from my boring, low-keyed everyday life. When I took the speed, I was outgoing and wanted to be around people; I did not have the feeling of fear in my soul. I liked the way the drug made me feel, like a self-starter, like the motivation to get me moving. I was fourteen when I started taking drugs, and speed was my drug of choice.

I would get them from my brother. I started hanging out with him even though he was seven years older than me. He would always say, "Come on, I am going to show you something." I thought he was going to show me something right then, he never did. He just took me everywhere he went, and I guess that is what he meant because I saw and learned much. He took me to hang out with his friends, who were all adults.

One night, I was stood at the top of the pasture and watched my sister come up the hill with two black men. When she got to the top of the hill, she introduced me to them, by saying, "This is my sister

Carolyn. Carolyn, this is Steve, my boyfriend, and his friend, David." I was like, "Wow, black people!" And such handsome black people! My sister's friends were well dressed; they looked as if they did not know anything about the country—no horses, no chickens, no cows. I looked like I did not know anything about handsome black men. There were only two black boys in my school, and they were so country, I thought they were white. They did not look like my sisters' friends. I was amazed.

The next time I met David, I was in Seattle at my sister's house. I was smitten with him, and he acted like he knew it, encouraging me to explore my feelings. I mean, he cornered me in the kitchen and asked to take me out. I was so flattered, so excited; I said, "Yes!" He was so good looking, oh my God, and he was twice my age. I said, "Who cares?" It seems my sister did. By the time my parents found out, we were in a relationship, and I was lost in love. I would run away from home, staying with him at the risk and peril of my parent's wrath. This was too much for my mother; she deemed me incorrigible, and I spent time in the youth detention center.

It was crazy I could not believe I was there. But that did not stop the relationship. David would write to me, using song lyrics, "Ain't no sunshine when you're gone, it's not warm when you're away. Ain't no sunshine when your gone, and you've been gone too long." He claimed, "When you get out it is going to be different." I was so excited to hear from him. I couldn't wait to see him.

When I was released, my father came to pick me up, saying, "We miss you! How are you?" And though I was so glad to see my father, I was anticipating seeing the one who said so many beautiful things to me. As soon as I got the chance, I was with him. He was warm; he was so concerned about how I had dealt with that experience. He said he would not let that ever happen to me again. I did not understand how much he meant he wanted to take care of me. Before I knew it, we were on our way to live in another city. The excitement was crazy, the adventure was thrilling, and I was with someone who I believe loved and cared for me.

Yet my adventure was not what I had expected, my excitement would soon be replaced with other emotions. We arrived in the city of Minneapolis, Minnesota, and when I found out that was where 'Prince' Roger Nelson was from, I was over the moon! And oh my God, the people were beautiful there. We settled into an apartment, and it was not long before my adventure transformed into a nightmare.

I was pregnant and terrified. David would be gone for days, leaving me uncertain about his whereabouts. As the days and nights alone passed, my baby grew, my body changed. I would stare in the mirror for long periods, just wondering what is happening in me. Sometimes I was happy and was comfortable with what I saw and sometimes fear would grip me, leaving me crying, wanting to talk to my mother. I called her, letting her know what was going on with me. I told her that David was not around much, fearing she would say, "I will send you a ticket to come home." And while I was afraid and alone, I couldn't come home; I didn't want to.

♛

As I lay in bed alone one night, I begin to feel a terrible pain in my back. I woke to see blood between my legs, my heart dropped. I begin to panic. I raised myself from the bed, blood was everywhere, tears filled my eyes, and I begin to cry, "Mama!" I rushed to the bathroom, holding my stomach. I was six months along in my pregnancy; my heart was palpitating. I couldn't reach David, and I was alone. As the pain increased, I fell to the floor. As I tried to stand, I slipped in my blood; the fear intensified. Crawling back to the bedroom, I stayed on my knees for a while, not knowing what to do. Again, came a sharp pain. Grabbing my stomach, I screamed, "Help me! Help me!" Finally reaching the phone, I called 911, saying, "I don't know what is happening to me, can you send me an ambulance."

I was drowning in tears, my heart racing; the pain was becoming unbearable. By the time the ambulance came, I was laying on the floor, exhausted. When the male EMTs began to remove my bloody gown, I was ashamed. I remember saying, "Please don't do that," the man said, "Lady, we have to look," and my heart dropped again.

I closed my eyes; when I opened them again, I was in the hospital. I laid there, in pain, wondering what was happening. I raised myself up and felt tremendous pain. I screamed, which summoned a nurse who asked, "Are you ok, can I help you." In tears and embarrassed, I asked, "What is happening to me?" She didn't give me any details but quickly left the room, telling me to wait. She returned with a bag of blood and started hooking me up to it. I asked again, "What is happening to me?"

"You have lost a lot of blood, and we will have to give you a blood transfusion." I began to shiver profusely; I was cold all over. The nurse apologized, "I am sorry we did not have time to warm the blood." She left to get me more blankets. I was horrified. I asked if I could call my mother, and she asked if I could wait, they needed to examine me further.

It was so cold in that room. As the doctor began to examine me, my embarrassment was overwhelming; I began to cry. The doctor said, "I am so sorry your baby didn't make it. It has died of strangulation from the umbilical cord. My heart sunk again, and I thought I was going to die. I needed to talk to my mother. The doctor said, "Right now, we will have to take steps to induce labor." I did not know what he was talking about; all the time he was talking, he was touching me and feeling around. When he left the room, I looked down at the foot of the bed and saw a string tied to the bed. When I asked the nurse, "What is that string for?" She coldly replied, "It is tied to the fetus until we induce labor." I could take no more and began to feel like I was losing myself. While I screamed and cried for my mother, she told me I need to rest while they prepared to induce labor. I began to scream again, so she gave me something to help me rest.

I awoke to a nurse looking at me and saying, "How are you doing?" She began to explain that they had taken the fetus out and that if I want to see it, I could. I said, "Yes, yes, I do." When they brought it to me, my heart was crushed. I asked about the gender; they told me he was a boy.

As they left the room, I asked again if I could please call my mother, and they finally gave me the approval to make a long-distance call. As I spoke to my mother, all I could say is, "Mom, I am in the hospital." She asked, "Are you ok?" I said, "Yes," and I could say no more. Then I heard the words I need most, "Do you want me to send you a ticket to come home?"

Thirty years later, the pain of that experience surfaced again. And as I mourned the death of my son, I realized he was still with me, and that I had not given him a name. I realized my baby boy was nameless and was still waiting for me to embrace him and remember him as my first born.

Today I thank my heavenly Father for bringing healing to my heart, at a time when I could handle the experience of that pain again and walk through it with forgiveness and love in my heart. I am grateful for the opportunity to name my baby boy and embrace him as my first born. David Elijah Aden Johnson, I love you.

KIMBERLY SUAZO-VALENTIN

Bonded by Brokenness

I am often told that I have so much potential to do great and amazing things. "Emerita, you are beautiful, and you will inspire so many young girls!" "How does it feel to be chosen, girl? You will do so many great things in the future. Man, you're so young, just imagine where God will take you when you are my age." In theory, it sounds beautiful; however, I have never felt that way. When I looked at myself, I felt what I saw was distorted; I longed to see what others saw in me. I felt trapped in my own bondage.

Nah. You're wrong. I just know how to finesse and make it <u>look</u> like I am successful.

In reality, every day, I get up in the morning, and I put on a 'mask' of perfection. I become the person that everyone wants me to be. I become the daughter that is independent and responsible. I become the employee that is a team player. I become the friend that you can vent to and unload your life struggles without worrying about your business being told. I become the person that everyone needs. However, no one knows the truth about me. The truth is I hate myself. I do not *feel* like I am worthy of love and affection. I do not *feel* like I am beautiful, and I sure as hell do not *feel* like I have the power to inspire any damn body.

I long for love and affection so much that I accept it anyway that I can get it. The truth is I am addicted to cycles of unhealthy relationships. I desire affection so much that I entertained anyone that comes my way. Mostly, because I am unsure if I will ever get attention again.

I am desperate. A good friend once told me, "Rita, when are you going to stop picking up those 'stray dogs?'" But *I* feel like a stray dog, and if stray dogs are the only ones that show me the love that I desire, I am going to take it. I feel I need them, and they need me.

♛

Since I was a young girl, I never truly felt like I deserved the world. Settling for less felt more like the cards that I was dealt. "You get what you get, and you do not throw a fit," was a saying that I lived by. My mother learned how to deal with her pain in silence by watching my grandmother mutely survive in an abusive relationship after abusive relationship. When you witness your mom dealing with her pain silently, you adopt those same coping strategies.

I learned how to deal with my pain alone because that is just the way women dealt with trauma in my family. My father was not faithful during my parents' marriage, but my mom remained in a dysfunctional marriage to complete the perfect picture. He cheated on her several times, yet my mom was a loyal and dedicated woman who was committed to her family.

My parent's relationship was my first example of what I could expect in a romantic partnership. My mom showed me that in a relationship, you must overcompensate to please your man. You must know how to cook, clean, and support your man. Your job is to uplift him and be his cheerleader, no matter the cost. As long as a man needs you, you are in the right place.

I had vivid memories when I was about eight years old of my mom getting home after a long day of work, she would race to the kitchen to prepare a quick and hearty meal for my father; while he laid on the couch and wait. "Men will be men," was the saying that repeated in my household. As long as the man is providing financially and laying down the pipe, then there was no reason to complain. At least that is what I thought was right.

As I grew older, my addiction to feeling worthless increased. My negative self-talk only got louder, and any words of affirmation offered by others felt like a delusion. My experiences and the ones before me were constant reminders that I had no alternatives. Be what a man needs, accept what comes your way, or die alone. I refused to die alone.

Eighteen Years Later…

"Omw to your crib," Jarron text rapidly as he left Azule Lounge, a popular nightclub in Houston, Texas.

Welp, let's see how this shit goes. Don't be awkward Emerita, Jarron is cool as hell!

Jarron was a good ass time. It's been about a year and a half since I last saw him. I met Jarron after leaving the Uptown Hookah Lounge back in 2015. My sorority sisters and I were attending a National Convention for our illustrious sorority, Delta Sigma Theta Sorority Incorporated. By day, we were attending preliminary workshops and handling our Delta business, and by night, we were the Redz, proudly yelling, *"Ooo-ooop!"* and strolling in venues.

After a night filled with laughs, drinks, and good music, we rally up to head home.

"It says he is here, but I don't see him." Marie expels loudly.

"Call and see real quick," Iesha insisted

This Uber better hurry up! This low key looks like the hood. I don't want to be here if anything pops off!

"They canceled, bro!" Marie exclaimed.

"Forreal, bro," I scuffed

"Ayye, ya'll need a ride? My line brother and I can take you if you want!"

Jarron gazed at our struggle from afar and came to our rescue. He was a 29-year-old graduate from Texas State University and was one of the Bruhz, a member of Omega Psi Phi Fraternity Incorporated. Jarron was tall with an athletic, muscular build. His line brother had braids, was short in stature, and looked like he came out of the movie *Friday*. My sorority sisters and I side-eyed each other, to make sure we all approved, and then we all said in harmony, "Hell Yeah!"

Southern hospitality was a beautiful experience for a West Coast girl like me. That night, and for the remainder of our stay in Houston, we became well acquainted with Jarron and his line brother. Jarron is the Bruhz, so he knows how to entertain. The Bruhz are known for being nasty "Q Dawgs." Besides, they are known for being pillars in their communities as teachers, role models, football players, and coaches.

Jarron was humorous and charming. He was a teacher at a high school and truly enjoyed what he did. He enjoyed giving back to his community. That night he "set it out" and sung many of the Bruhz infamous vulgar chants for us to record on our Snap-Chats. During the drive, we all shared positive energy and free-flowing conversation about whatever came to our drunken minds.

"Where ya'll Redz from?" Jarron asked.

"Washington. We're the traveling Redz," we eagerly replied.

I visited Houston often to spend time with my mom. Since I live in Seattle, I do not have the luxury of seeing her every day. Moving to Houston in 2014, I made a conscious effort to spend quality time with my mom, especially during the holiday season.

It was a bright sunny day in December of 2017, being in Houston meant taking full advantage of the Southern Hospitality that surrounded me. The men in the south recognize a queen when they see one.

"Ma! I'll be back later. I'm going out with my friend," I said.

"Who is your friend, and how do you know them?" my mom probed in a thick Spanish accent.

"I met him the last time I was here. He is a part of my brother Fraternity Ma," her prying annoyed me.

MA! I'm grown. Let me have fun, I thought.

Facetime Call from Jarron:

"Hey," I answer doing my best to hold my composure.

"Ayye! I'm outside."

"Aight, I'm coming."

Before leaving, I tell my mom that I love her and reassure her that I will be back later. Jarron and I skirt off to the ghetto of Houston in search of some "fire." Too bad we could only get our hands on some "Reggie," the worst quality weed known to man.

We parked in a quiet yet skeptical neighborhood. Jarron began to roll up the Reggie, and together we temporarily escaped our realities. With each puff, I could feel my body become more relaxed, and my mind becomes less anxious. We conversed for hours about our lives and the struggles of being black in America. The present, the past, and the future.

"What is the lesson that you learned in your last relationship?" I asked.

He paused than responded, "My ex was wifey material, but I was young. I did not want to be tied down. I cheated. I know that the next relationship that I enter, I will be ready, but for right now, I am living my life."

"Why do men cheat when they have a good woman, that shit doesn't make any sense."

He chuckles, "To be honest because ain't no pussy, like new pussy."

Damn, that's fucked up. I want to cuss you out for saying something so off the wall, You are lucky you are cute though, I think to myself as I admired his honesty.

I would be lying if I did not admit I wished he were ready to settle down. He was perfect! He and I shared a common love for youth. We both worked at a high school with at-risk youth. We recognized that the kids we mentored were smarter than what society gave them credit for. We felt it was our responsibility to plant seeds in the youth for them to develop greatness within themselves.

The moments we shared were similar to the lyrics of the song *Pretty Little Fears* by 6LACK featuring J.Cole. We were vulnerable to one another. We shared past wounds, current fears, and future goals.

Is this the same nigga that sent me those enticing dick pics last night?

Jarron was a black man with perspective. He realized he had a responsibility as a black man. He was aware that because he is a black man, the police were going to be twice as hard on him, which is why he had the uber sticker on his car window.

A lot of black men are in jail, and their sons have no one to turn to, so they turn to the streets. Jarron works daily to be a positive influence on his students. I shared with him that I feel the influence I have is too small when comparing the adversity that the child is experiencing. Jarron responds,

"How small is a mustard seed, Rita?"

Most people called me Rita for short because they did not know how to pronounce Emerita. I smiled, while also giving him an annoyed side eye, reluctantly saying, "You're right…"

Wow! This nigga is lit.

He continues, "And in the Bible, it says that's all you need to move a mountain. Have faith that God will use those times to inspire them to overcome their adversities."

I did not think the conversation was going to be that good. He is so engaging! I thought he was going to try to press the issue and be much nastier, especially with that dick pic he sent me last night…

Do not play yourself Emerita. If Jarron sent that dick pic to you, he probably sent it to hella other bitches, you ain't nobody special. Remember, he is not looking for anything serious relationships because he is still "living his life." You want marriage, he does not. You deserve more than just a smoke session and a conversation. But, good company ain't never hurt nobody…

Jarron was just that, good company for the moment. Although we had a lot in common, I knew that we were not going anywhere. He was a part of my brother fraternity, so he was essentially showing me hospitality. He was nice. The reality was that he did not want anything serious. I was traveling, so I was not too disappointed in the outcome; however, I also wished that moment it lasted a lifetime. Nonetheless, I was determined to continue to live my best life in Houston.

Welp, there are more men in Houston, let me enjoy my vacation, I told myself.

"Good Boy, Kingston! Let's go, you're doing so good!" The Houston shined on my sister's dog, and I. Kingston rarely goes on walks, so when cars drive by, he stops walking and squats on the ground. I encouraged him to continue forward. I needed to get out of the house and get some fresh air. My mom was having one of her overbearing moments.

Being one of the youngest in the family has its pros and cons, and one of the cons is my mom treats me as if I am a child, even though I am 26 years old. To revitalize my energy, I chose to go on a walk. Kingston was my chosen company. Walking we passed Flamingo Drive, Beldart St, Westover St, Belmark St, Belarbor St, and back around to Sharondale Drive. I enjoyed the sun, as I walk the streets unbothered in an orange bonnet with Kingston, the Rottweiler beside me.

Many of the homes were not fenced with unleashed dogs in the yard. One dog quickly stood up in defense as Kingston, and I walked by.

"Emerita, what the fuck were you thinking walking Kingston? This ain't Seattle. People do not walk their dogs in the hood, now your ass is about to get attacked by this Pitbull!"

With quick and swift feet, I passed by the alert Pitbull and sighed with relief as I realized we were a few blocks away from the house. As I got closer, I noticed a man in a questionable van attempting to get my attention.

"Oh, hell, no. He better keep driving. I am not in the mood to have no conversation," I scowled.

He looked like he had a mechanic job. His face was sweaty, and his shirt fit loose on his body. Driving in the opposite direction, he abruptly turns the van around and slows down to approach me.

"How is ya doing lil lady? What's ya name?" he asked with a deep southern accent.

Who does he think he is stopping me in this trifling looking ass van? He must be confident in himself, cause what is this shit?

"Rita, what's your name?"

"Byron"

"Where you are coming from Byron? You're all, sweaty!" I was always a bit bolder in my interaction with men when I was traveling.

"I just got off work, I work for a moving company. This is my work van."

Okay, nigga!

"I am visiting my mother for a holiday."

"Can I get your number? I want to see you before you leave."

Do not give this man your number, he has been looking at your boobs and butt the whole time ya'll been talking and he ain't even all that cute. But you are not looking cute either sis, with your orange bonnet. You lucky anybody even stopped you to see what's up with you, my inner voice raved.

"(206) 555-9988."

"Alright, Ill text you later."

Byron was a simple man. He was born and raised in the hood of Sunnyside, now thirty-five years old; he was working odd jobs to help his mom. She had cancer. Between him and his brother, Byron was more responsible and maintained the family business. When I talked to Byron, he never had much to say. His answers were always brief, engaging conversation definitely was not his strength.

Byron was a hood booger, meaning a person from the hood that has embodied a poverty mindset because of his negative experiences. Byron was exposed to gun violence and death at the age of eight. He witnessed his father get shot because a "friend" set him up. Byron had to grow up fast to help provide food for his family. There was a daily struggle to provide meals. He did what he knew best, selling drugs. Byron was a product of his environment; he was from the streets. Since he witnessed death and violence, he eventually grew numb to it.

He was constantly in survival mode and aimlessly living his life. Byron did not have short or long-term goals. He was breathing air, one day at a time, patiently waiting on his last days to draw near. Nevertheless, everyone has gifts. Byron might have been a hood booger, but he knew how to please a woman.

"I'm outside," I look down at my phone to see Byron's text. After dodging Byron for days, I finally decided to give him some attention. Byron sold weed, and I was inquiring. He offered to give me a sample before I bought some and I gladly accepted the kind gesture. I came out in a black bonnet with my personalized Seahawks blanket wrapped around me. He rolled a healthy blunt, and together we inhaled the THC and transcended to cloud nine. Quietly beaming at me with his darting eyes, he looked at me as if he had been waiting on this moment for some time now. With his lips puckered, he leaned in for a kiss.

Playing hard to get, I respond, "I never said you could kiss me."

I was curious to see what this man had up his sleeve. I think I was *too* curious, though. It was as if Byron knew all the answers to the test, and I was the test. He knew exactly what to do. The vibe felt like the song, *Body* by Dreezy featuring Jeremiah. I was convinced that I was about to catch a body. It had been a while since I felt sexually comfortable with a man.

I barely knew Byron, but the way Byron circulated his tongue around my nipple, while simultaneously fingering me in the back of the minivan, made me feel like we had known each other for a lifetime. If lust had a look, it looked exactly like what we were doing. Stroking each other's lustful spirits, both of us longing for fulfillment by instant gratification in a minivan outside my mamas' house.

"Really!?," Byron would whine in his deep southern accent when I refused to let him go all the way.

This feels super bomb, but I can't let this nigga fuck. How the hell did I get myself in this situation? Why did you give him your number in the first place? Did you forget that he is a hood booger and has a limited perspective? Emerita you are a college graduate you are smarter than this. You are entertaining a man with no substance. A man that has nothing going for themselves, besides having a sexual experience. When are you going to learn Emerita? DO BETTER!

I knew that I did not have enough strength to do better. Being frustrated was not enough for me to change my ways. I could scrutinize Byron as much as I wanted, but that did not change the fact that I felt the desire to entertain him. His story compelled me to remind him that he was not alone and that even though he had a poverty mindset, I wanted him to know that I saw him, and I thought he was a King. I realized that I was addicted to being a sex object, so much so that I would perpetuate the very thing I hated. He did not need to get to know me, because he was giving me the attention, I thought I needed. Each touch made me feel beautiful, loved, and chosen, but I knew in my heart that a lustful and lonely spirit connected us.

The remainder of my trip was enjoyable and spent with family. I decided to take a break from the male gaze and attempt to focus on myself. Why did I have such low expectations when it came to men? Why did I pity myself? And, where did these feelings of inadequacy come from? I did not know the answer to this question, but after that night with Byron, I knew I had to start being real with myself if I wanted to see any *change* in myself.

Nine months later...

"Oooweee, hold it down, Baby Zeke!" I exclaimed cheerfully. Ezekiel was a beast on the football field. Every opportunity he had; he would tackle the players on the opposing team that tried to step to him. He was nobody to play with on the field. I stood in the stands like a proud parent, smiling from ear to ear, because he was accomplishing the dreams that he always had as a young boy—to play football in college then go to the NFL. He played on the Roos Field, better known as the "Inferno" for the Eastern Washington Eagles. When he gave me the news that he could finally play after his academic probation and injuries, I opened my schedule and made a trip to Eastern Washington University to pay my old friend a visit.

I grew up with Ezekiel in West Seattle; he was like my little brother. His mother had five kids, three boys, and two girls. Ezekiel was the oldest. I met the family when they moved into the neighborhood from South Central, Los Angeles. I was sixteen, and Ezekiel was eleven. We instantly clicked because of our similar sense of humor.

"Whoever loses this Uno Game is a rotten egg and has to crack an egg on their butt," I would contest.

"Bet! Rita, you suck anyway!"

Fun family games and quality time helped us get our mind off our current adversity of being from poor working-class families. I would often go over to his house and "put him on game" about life (or at least what I knew and experienced). I would constantly encourage him to stay focused in school so that he could accomplish his football dreams. Ezekiel had a passion for football, and as someone that believed in him and wanted to support his vision; I was determined to be the consistent person in his corner rooting him on.

He had several responsibilities at a young age, so me being an empathetic person, I naturally felt for Ezekiel, because he was born into a predicament, too common to the black man's story. Ezekiel had no positive male guidance in his life because his father was absent. Raised by his mother and grandmother, Ezekiel was to be a role model for his younger siblings, but he did not have anyone to look to for guidance. He loved his siblings and did everything in his power to influence them positively. Being a single mother, Ezekiel's mother was not always able to attend his games, so I made sure that whenever I could go, I was there, supporting Ezekiel. He played for the West Seattle Wildcats Junior football team from ages eleven to fourteen, then played varsity for West Seattle High school. While I was in college, we always remained in contact and stayed close friends.

Ezekiel was now twenty-one years old playing defensive end for Eastern Washington University. I was so proud of him and all his hard work. Many people doubted him, but he made it.

"Ayyyyyye, let's go Eagles! I see you # 77 Let's goooo!" I cheered. On September 1st of 2018, Eastern Washington won against Central Washington University fifty-eight to thirteen.

"I see you out there! You're still using them corny moves I see," I joked.

He quickly clapped back, "Aight! They're corny, but they work every time, right?"

We always understood each other. People always viewed me as aggressive. Other men I would meet would often make comments that were harsh with my words or not 'ladylike.' Ezekiel knew me though, we came from the same struggle, and so what was understood did not need to be explained. We always played rough, but it was all in love.

"I guess you did sack that Quarterback or whatever. Why do you got to be such a showoff, Baby Zeke?"

"Yeah, I sacked that nigga three times, I know you saw that! Did you get it on Snap Chat? And stop calling me that, I'm grown now, Rita. Ya boy is legal now, so you better put some respect on my name, girl."

Hell yeah, you're grown now. Damnnn Baby Zeke, your low-key fine now! Looking like a whole snack! I know we grew up together, but you're grown now, and I'm trying to see what's up

Ezekiel had a husky build yet was muscular. He was 6'3 and weighed 250 pounds. He had a dark caramel complexion, long voluptuous locs, and a gorgeous white smile that was blinding, yet when you looked into his eyes, they were dismissive.

"Yea I got it on Snap Chat, big head," I ignored the comment he made.

"Let's celebrate this dub now. I am proud of you! I brought cookies to roll up, a bottle of Hennessey, groceries for dinner, and this Uno game. Are you ready to get your ass beat? You might be dope at football, but I got Uno all day! The loser is a rotten egg!"

"Let's go! Rita, you know you suck, stop playing."

We both laughed and ran to the car as if we were young again, then headed to his apartment. Ezekiel was very quiet and reserved. He maintained a calm demeanor throughout most of life's circumstances. Once, when he was sixteen, some kids robbed him as he was passed through South Seattle. Although he didn't gangbang, they saw his West Seattle High School Jersey and immediately bum rushed him. When he told me about it, his response was, "It's okay, Rita. That's life, but how has college life been treating you?" He did not trust many people, but he trusted me, so I did not take my position in his life lightly.

He trusted me. However, he had moments when he was reserved and did not want to talk about his deep fears and concerns. He did not have many friends in college, besides his teammates. He was cool with many people; however, He did not allow people into his personal life. It took time to gain Ezekiel's trust since he could sense bullshit from a mile away. I knew he needed me during this time, so I was determined to support him, even if it meant pausing my own life for a while to visit him. His roommates all had plans, so we had the apartment to ourselves for the night.

As we arrived at the apartment, I scurried to the kitchen to start making dinner. At that moment, I had a quick flashback of when my mother would do the very same thing for my father when I was younger. I became my mother. Through observations, I learned to be what a man needs out of fear of being alone— there were no alternatives.

"I bought your fav, Zeke!"

"Steak and potatoes?! Rita, you definitely know the way to a man's heart." Ezekiel flirtatiously remarked, looking directly into my eyes and soul.

This boy better stop before I pounce on him. He will escape the friend zone real quick, looking at me like that.

I laughed with flatter and responded, "I've been making this since we were younger. Everybody got to eat, Baby Zeke. I'll let you know when it's ready. Go away so that I can focus."

Ezekiel grinned and made his way to his room. While he was playing Madden nineteen, I started to cook the food. It did not take very long to make since I seasoned the meat earlier. About forty-five minutes later, I had a full course meal, and it was ready to serve with Hennessy and Coca-Cola for our beverages. Before we ate, we 'hot boxed' the bathroom, so that we could *really* enjoy the food.

Together we entered into a land of no worries, experiencing feelings of lightness where unwanted distraction faded into the background.

"So how has Eastern been treating you? You got a boo yet?"

"It's cool; I do what I have to do to play. Being on academic probation really put everything into perspective for me. Rita, you know I am not worried about these Thotianas (hoes). They just like me cause of what I do on the field, but they ain't really for me."

"I feel it! Well, that's what's up. I am glad you are figuring everything out. Do not worry, the woman that you end up with will be lucky. You grew up to become a very handsome man, Baby Zeke."

"I am not worried about all of that right now. I have to focus on this football. Shit, I don't even know if I want to get married."

Damn. Why?! Shit, marry my ass, Ezekiel. We would have the most bomb babies ever. We would be a dynamic couple I just know it. We have known each other for a longtime, and I can be that woman that you need. I have supported your football journey since you were a kid, and I will continue to support you. Why won't he see that I am the woman that he needs? However, is he the man that I need?

"Really? Why not? I want to get married. I am twenty-six years old, and I am only getting older. One day I want to have kids and be married to the man that God has for me. I don't want to be dating all my life."

"God?" he scuffed. "I feel like Christianity is a religion for slavery. They used the bible to keep our people in bondage for years. But, if marriage and kids are what you want, then I believe you will find it. Emerita, you are beautiful inside and out. Shit, anybody that has you is lucky! You are so successful at such a young age, inspiring the kids that you work with, just imagine where you will be in ten years. You a boss girl!" He voice was sincere.

Did this nigga just say that he did not believe in God? We used to go to church together all the time. Man, that conversation is for a whole other day, the food is getting cold. Man fuck,

I wish we were on the same page because we would be so perfect for each other.

"Not my government name though," I poked. "Thank you, Baby Zeke, that means a lot," I tried to contain my smile.

"Let's go eat, I got the munchies now. I know you were throwing down too because I could smell it from my room. Thank you for coming through Rita, I appreciate you forreal," Zeke ushered me to the dinning area.

"You know I got you! Let's go eat."

We indulge in the miraculous dinner that I made, sipped on our mixed drinks, and continued our conversation. We updated each other on our families, shared our future aspirations, and disclosed where we saw ourselves in the next ten years. We played back-to-back games of Uno until he won more times than I did because he is a sore loser.

After hours of fun and banter, we eventually went to sleep in his room using separate blankets, like, we used to do growing up. Throughout the day, our words were innocent and friendly, but our body language was flirtatious. Ezekiel brushed passed me a few times, holding on to my hips. I would respond by pushing my rear against him, feeling his semi-hard penis. The vibe felt like *Body Language* by Kid Ink featuring Usher. We did not have to say too much, because we were reading each other body language. You could feel the sexual tension in the room;

however, neither one of us were bold enough to make the first move while the lights were on.

We fell asleep for a few hours, and then I woke up randomly and decided to shoot my shot. With liquor courage still in my system, I slowly inched my way into his blanket. One thing led to another, and the next thing I knew, he was going down on me. It was an element of surprise.

Owwwee, this feel bomb. He sure ain't a baby anymore. WAIT! What are we doing? We done opened up a can of worms. Here you go again, Emerita! When will you learn your lesson?

"Dammnnnn," I moaned.

STOP Emerita! What are you thinking? He is twenty-one, and you are twenty-six. You want to get married, and Ezekiel is still trying to figure things out in his life. Why do you keep doing this to yourself? Giving men the time of day, when you are not a priority. However, he understands me, and it feels so good to be loved and understood.

We ended the oral sex prematurely and instead engaged in making out foreplay, then cuddled each other back to sleep. The morning after was a little awkward because we crossed a boundary in our friendship. However, we never discussed it and continued our relationship. We both knew it was for the best.

That morning, we went to brunch, and I packed my car to head back home to Seattle. I was sick of being in this cycle of being a man's "just for now." I felt invisible and belittled. I knew I deserved more, but I did not know how to manifest it. I had to come to terms with my behaviors. One day I looked in the mirror and asked myself hard questions:

Why were these kind of men a reoccurring theme in my life? Why did I constantly accept being the "in the moment" vibe with a man rather than being a man's lifetime?

How was I able to fully manage my job, finances, and overall responsibilities so well, yet when it came to my love life, it was always wavering. I had to take a deep look at myself and share the ugly truth. I realized that I was trying to be the woman that I observed my mother be. I accepted the men that resembled my father in one way or another. Throughout my life, I observed and displayed what *I* felt my role was as a woman and internalized that the men who came my way were the best I could do.

Again, my inner voice spoke, *Emerita, you have daddy issues. Big time.* The reality was a hard pill to swallow. I craved what I was used to 'eating' because it seemed normal. I had a hunger and a thirst for validation from a man, even if it met shrinking myself to fit into their lifestyle. I needed them to see that I was worth loving. I wanted them to remind me that I am good enough.

Jarron, you are an intelligent and strong black man, but commitment is not a priority to you, just like my father. We can exchange dialogue so effortlessly for hours, but I know that I am just a booty call. I recognize that I deserve more than this. God has plans for me to prosper. I acknowledge that I deserve better. I finally choose my healing.

Byron, I am empathetic of all the adversity that you had to overcome. Life has dealt you a fucked-up deck of cards. Like my father, you have been a provider for your family, but your limiting perspective is blocking you from your blessing. There is more to life than Sunnyside, and I know that my future will require a man that can fulfill me past sexual pleasures. With the goals and dreams that I have for my future, I acknowledge that I will need a man that can support and push me further into my purpose. Receiving instant gratification feels good, but I need something more long-lasting. Proverbs 3:15 says that I am more precious than rubies, so it is about time that *I* start acting like it. I acknowledge that I deserve better, and I finally choose my healing.

Ezekiel, you are one of my closest friends. We grew up together, and we have been through so much. You've defied the odds that were against you and made it. However, we are at different stages in our lives. I want to be married. If we were together, I would sacrifice myself to validate your needs, and that is unacceptable. I am learning that God is the only one that affirms me. Sometimes I think of how perfect we would be together, but we are unequally yoked. I pray one day you heal, but I acknowledge that I deserve better, and I finally choose my healing.

Our struggles connected us, and we were bonded by our brokenness. Each puff-puff-pass relieved us from our cruel reality, but only for a while. It was a bandage to cover up the pain, but when the high when down, we still had our brokenness to attend.

I had to realize that two of the same things could never be fruitful. I constantly denied myself for the satisfaction of others. I felt like if a man needed me that meant that I had the privilege of being with him. Our relationship revealed that I was mirroring what my mother did to keep my father happy; accepting what she did not deserve. I was doing the same thing but hoping for a different result.

When I look at each of you, I see your potential. Jarron, Byron, and Ezekiel, all of you, are Kings, Kings trapped in bondage. I pray that one day, you see yourself as Kings and heal. However, I must choose myself this time. As a healing Queen, I am learning that my job in a relationship is to be a helpmate, not a servant.

People say that the truth will set you free, and, I Emerita Rodriguez is ready to be free!" As I face my reflection, tears rush down my face like a flowing stream. From this day forward, I will not live in bondage, my chains are finally broken.

NORMA GONZÁLEZ

Monsters

When you've been exposed to monsters, the reality that they exist weighs heavy on your conscious, if you have one. I mean it's always a choice, right? To become like the monster or run like hell the other way. But what if its more complicated than that? What if you can't choose and despite how much you try, a little bit of that monster lives and grows inside of you. Maybe you try to be better, whatever "better" means to you. But instead, those survival tactics come across as irrational behavior, self-preservation comes across as selfish, and love comes across as rage. Can you have monsters and still be normal? What is normal after you've been exposed to monsters?

My mother was raised by a monster. Her father beat the child out of her at a young age. She was one of eight children working in the fields for a family paycheck. My brother, sister, and I grew up hearing about this monster. We decided to hate him, despite my mother's lessons on forgiveness and his yearly visits to act as a grandfather when we knew what he was.

My mom would tell us how he pulled her out of school to take care of her younger siblings. How she raised kids when she was just a kid herself and how she "never wanted kids." She would remind us how lucky we were to go to school and not have to work. When we got in trouble, she would tell us how he used to beat her "like a grown man," leaving her bloody and blue for days. "I wouldn't do that to you guys," she would tell us.

Instead, my father would beat us- with a belt, not his fist, and never for too long or without a good reason, otherwise she would panic and go into a fit of screams and tears. We grew up understandably confused, but we had each other to remind ourselves that something was wrong with *her*, not us. *We just need to leave her alone and stop making her angry*, we thought.

In my twenties, the old man died, complicated surgery and misdiagnosis caused him to deteriorate from a 200 pound 6-foot-tall cowboy hat wearing Tejano; to a brittle pile of brown bones. The day of the funeral, all my mother's siblings showed up, even the uncle who was on the run, and the aunt who swore off the family in exchange for her Lord and Savior. I had never seen them all in one room.

The day was a blur of Tejano rage, crying strangers we had never met, and confused children. When the program started, my mother quickly grabbed the mic from the minister. Exposing her puffy red face and thick tears, she scolded everyone in the room for not being more united, for showing up for the funeral to save face, but not showing up at the hospital during the six months he was dying. She had been the only one in the family to go to the hospital every day, despite our own protests of confusion.

"Why are you taking care of him after everything he did to you?" my older brother finally asked. "Because he's still my father," she responded with rage choking back tears.

It's hard growing up seeing someone you love in pain and not being able to take it away. As a kid, I was always getting sick and being taken to the hospital for my bad kidneys. I saw my mother struggle to balance a full-time job, my father's needs, my troublemaking siblings, and my medical diagnosis. I always felt guilty for making her work harder. I did my best to stay quiet and avoid making her mad. As an adult, I still try hard to avoid making her upset. I only tell her the good things: "I got a new job," not I'm homeless and don't have anywhere to stay.

I became a social worker because I wanted to understand my mother. I worked with women in abusive relationships, some who had come from abused homes like my mother had. The stories were intense and gave me nightmares. Aside from my mother's stories, I had never heard about so much abuse. I thought my mother's life story was rare, I quickly found out it wasn't. My mother and I talked about my job and the barriers that the women faced and sometimes the stories if she asked. We talked about abusive men and toxic masculinity, and we learned from each other. She began to soften up during those talks.

One day I invited her out to breakfast with my friends from work. The breakfast quickly turned into a full-on therapy session. Four trained victim advocates and none of us could say anything to comfort her that day. She told us through tears about the way he treated her. How she got it worse than her younger siblings because she was always home. How, despite how he treated her, she still loved him because she wanted a father. How she cared for him in the hospital when no one else would, and how he never even bothered to thank her before he died. The way she told this story was different. She wasn't emotionless or angry, her two default emotions growing up. She was expressing a range of emotions. When she finished, she finally admitted, without directly saying it, that there was something wrong with *him*, not her. He was the monster, not her.

Soon after, I left social work and went to law school. I realized the problem was big, so I wanted to help in a grander way. What better way than lawyering? But for a poor brown first generation college kid, it's not as easy as just getting the degree. I saw bigger systemic problems rather than individual client problems. I saw racism play out in the cases I read for class that I couldn't ignore like the white students. The apathy I faced in school forced me out into the streets. I began attending protests and getting involved in activist circles. I got in touch with my inner angry brown girl.

The desire to do more than the monsters in power, got the best of me when Trump happened. I was attending law school part-time, working full time, and going to community events in between homework. My rage pushed me through law school, but also pushed me to my limits. It took two miscarriages to finally wake me up and realize that I wasn't living my life; I was burning myself alive. I wanted so much to change things that I was willing to sacrifice myself. I wanted people to understand how ugly this world really is and give others the same sense of urgency that I felt, which was constant and suffocating.

I stopped working so hard because the stories did something to me. They live inside me now, fueling this rage I can't seem to let go of. It's like the monster my mother was able to fight off, lives in me now. My mother tells people her daughter is an immigration lawyer in Seattle, but the truth is I'm unemployed and stuck.

My stomach churns itself into a knot whenever I enter a court room because I know there is no justice when these stories still exist. The thought of respecting a judge whose bias determines the future of an individual who looks like me takes my rage to places I'm too scared to enter. Not actively seeking a job is coming off as irrational, avoiding circles that ignite my anger is self-preservation, but it comes across as selfish, and my love for people comes across as irrational rage. Can you have monsters and still be normal? What is normal when you live amongst monsters?

ANITA KOYIER-MWAMBA

Wealth and Sensibility

It started out as a wonderful sunny day, full of love. As was customary, I ran to Mama and Baba's bed for my good morning ritual of songs and tickles. Nothing stood out particularly. It must have been a weekend, but I don't recall exactly what day. I was five years old. As always, after I bid them good morning, I ran to the bathroom to brush my teeth and wash my face. I donned my Bruce Lee t-shirt and jeans and waited patiently for the neighborhood children.

The day moved along, and we children headed to complete our nighttime ablutions, and change into our pajamas. I woke up to what sounded like a giant thud in the middle of the night. Another thud, another, and then I heard mama cry out. Fred, our brave, short, eight-year- old first-born older brother, jumped out of bed to investigate. His beautiful, big brown eyes, alert and fearless communicated to my brother Martin and I, to stay put. Martin, only eleven months younger than Fred, wiry and tall, handsome with a cheeky twinkle in his eye acquiesced. Who was I, the baby and only girl, to disobey such clear directives?

Fred walked stealthily to the door and peeked into the corridor and towards the kitchen and the pantry and ran out, shouting, "Stop hitting my mother!" I remember feeling like I was shrinking, and the room was getting bigger. Before that moment, I thought of us as five parts of one unit. At that moment, something major broke, and we became five individuals, connected by a common trauma, separated by our responses to it. I recall feeling like for the first time that something was fundamentally broken. Our fabulous five was more of our individual selves relating to what was left of the core.

The next thing I recall is Mama begging us to climb through the windows to her, but the windows were burglar proof. Fred tried to squeeze through the small window, but he couldn't. We were in our beautiful bedroom with modern double-decker beds. We pulled aside the curtains to see mama. The rose bushes outside our bedroom window were fragrant. Mama was elegant as always. High heeled boots, beautiful over the knee body hugging patterned dress and a large black purse. She gestured to the narrow window at the top and said, "Please come and I will catch you."

My brother climbed up the top bunk attempting to squeeze through the window to get to her. He was not able to. As a taxi arrived to pick her up, she was more frantic, sobbing outside in the front yard asking Baba to give her children. Her devastation was clear in her keening cries. Her distress haunts me to this day.

I walked into the living room where Baba sat with his big, lean six-foot-two frame seemingly relaxed on the sofa. His handsome brown face staring blankly until he noticed me. He gestured for me with his hand. He was profoundly sad. I walked to him, and he picked me up and spoke to me in such soothing, gentle tones. Reassuring me that all would be okay. I was his comfort. He was my assurance. Life was never the same again.

♛

I was five years old and motherless, and my dad was never home, I guess he was searching for his next wife. We were under very strict instructions not to let anyone into the house. Fred, my almost nine-year old brother, took such good care of us. He made sure we bathed and got into our beautiful pajamas. Mine was royal blue with a paisley pattern on them.

My mom would come by some nights with rotisserie chicken and fries when called. She asked us to promise not to tell my dad that she had been there. This pattern was sustained for a while. Before my sixth birthday, I was dealt with such a hard blow that it shook my world. My beloved, vivacious mom, full of joy and love, was arrested along with some business partners for selling large amounts of illegally acquired coffee beans. Shortly after I learned of her incarceration, an even bigger blow came my way.

We lost our home to auction. Our beautiful single-story home on half an acre of land. The floors were made of beautiful, gleaming white tile. The verandah at the front entrance was made of speckled yellow and black Italian Marble. I loved sitting and playing in that area. Adjacent to the verandah was a rose garden with sweet smelling red and yellow roses. But my favorite part of the house was the informal dining room with double French doors leading into the back yard.

There was an outdoor barbeque area and several fruit trees: pomegranate, mango, lemon, and lots of berry trees and bushes—loquats too. To the right of the garden were the garage and the servant's quarters. All along the drive to the garage were various tropical flowers and ferns. This was truly my favorite place to be. I was born and brought home to this house and thought I would get married there.

On that fateful day, all my dreams about our home turned to dust. You see, my dad had dabbled in politics and paid a terrible price. He lost his high-ranking office in government and was jobless for years. Those years were unkind. The first casualty was our home and its contents. I recall a detached curiosity about all the people walking through our home. I was by my dad's side through all of this.

Shortly after, we went to live with an uncle. My response to the trauma of losing our home was to tell myself that business was a dangerous enterprise because it sent my mother to prison. I also believed business as a profession to corrupt. When it fails, everything you own can be gone in a moment— leaving you destitute. Owning a grand home would result in losing it and that pain is unbearable.

Today I am a forty-eight-year-old mother of two who has some serious aversions to wealth accumulation. I live in a small two-bedroom house, with one bathroom. My house is cluttered and not a reflection of who I am. I have reached a place of grave discomfort with my lifestyle, struggles with trusting wealth, and desired lifestyle. I am blessed with so many gifts that it seems I am living an impostor's life.

Throughout my adulthood, I'd acquire beautiful things, always believing that I will lose them to forces beyond my control. The traumatic loss of my parent's marriage, our home, and lifestyle were things beyond my control. They happened to me without invitation or consent as a result of my parents' poor choices. The result is that I do not save, invest, or even routinely budget. The wound of loss is very tender.

As I write these words, I am aware of the illogical reasoning in my thinking. I also know that I am terrified of building great wealth just to lose it. I am determined to work through these wounds and find healing. These wounds from my fifth year of life continue to fester and are now impacting my quality of life and my relationships with people and to money.

In 1997, at the age of fifty-nine, my father died of a massive heart attack. He literally dropped dead on his way to a press conference. When he died, I was once more at the mercies of forces beyond my control. I was living in one of the homes he shared with my stepmom. To my shock, I was effectively removed from the home and told that I was not her child and that I did not have a place there.

At twenty-seven, I was back to being at the mercy of people who held practical power over me. Like a phoenix, I rose from those ashes to find my way back to the United States, the closest place to home that I have. The United States is where I became an adult and found my voice. I went to college and law school, found love, became conscious of my African self, and birthed my children. My rituals of life came to me here. Also, I live with less disease in the US than in other places.

In the end, Martin's personality was forever altered from vivacious extrovert he became a noticeable introvert. I became uncertain about my place in the family and the world, while Fred became a lover of people and material things. Martin disappeared at age twenty-nine, Fred died of HIV Aids complications at age twenty-seven, and me, I persist.

LINDA UPSHAW

Dare to be Free

"The universe, which is not merely the stars and the moon and the planets, flowers but other people, has evolved no terms for your existence, has made no room for you, and if love will not swing wide the gate, no other power will or can." --**James Baldwin**.

The sun was shining brightly that afternoon. It was summer in Manhattan, and I was happy. I felt so very blessed, that unlike most of my trips back to visit, that I found a place to stay where taxis regularly pass. It was the Upper West Side, and late summer. There were few street vendors around, but numerous grocery stores and restaurants of various ethnic groups. I had been planning on this particular excursion even before leaving my waterside home in Seattle. All that came before this moment, and cab ride, came streaming in, full bodied visible and vocal as in a surround sound movie. I had taken many such rides while living and working in Manhattan over thirty years ago, and after returning to Seattle. My mind would race with intrigue and mystery, not uncommon to those with my highly lucid imagination.

As I left my residence that afternoon, I stepped out into the busy street to hail a taxi. Several zoomed by, but the one that I needed glided right up to where I was standing. It was a simple and no stress activity compared to what I had been preparing to do for many years. I was on my way to view my late Uncle Charles' apartment. As I peered out of the window, I noticed that gentrification had not only taken over blocks of my old neighborhoods in Seattle but also in Harlem. Convenient stores, restaurants, beauty salons in the heart of Seattle's Central District are being replaced with apartment buildings where the rent is not affordable to residents in the area. Many of the foundational churches of this area, a stalwart in their support of the Civil Rights movement sixty years ago are being decimated. The population is fleeing to areas south of the Central District.

♛

I grew up in the very heart of the Central District. It was a village in every aspect. My mother would take us to her church circle meetings at a nearby resident's home. We would walk to the grocery store and take the bus to go downtown. People knew each other; it was a friendly village.

Our church and elementary school were both walking distance. We did not have a car until I was in middle school, so we were pretty much stuck in the house, with little activity except attending church and Sunday school, piano lessons, and homework. Because it was the fifties, and pre-civil rights, my sister and I were picked on endlessly because of our light skin. At that time, there was no Black Power or the Civil Rights Movement. Black was not considered "beautiful," and the kids in my elementary school ten minutes away felt demoralized. Teachers were insensitive. The story of "Little Black Sambo" was used as a children's literature story and read with abandon—I felt awful and aware that the other children did as well. Also, our mother made us wear orthopedic shoes, and made all our clothing, so we were very odd appearing, the fact that most classmates made sure we were aware of.

My mother's manner of childrearing was to be rigid. Her father, who lived in North Carolina, was a quiet man but abused his children – calling them names when he was out of sorts. Her mother was soft spoken and very reserved in her mannerisms. I had never met either one of them. No one questioned why he was that way – beyond an acknowledgement that he was intense - in the way that those with an artistic disposition are. He had very high standards and a great reputation in the area they lived – doing carpentry work. She had eight siblings, and they were all anxious to leave their home in North Carolina.

Our home was not a relaxed atmosphere, and we were guarded, checked, and restrained both inside the house and out. My father was gone from early in the morning to late at night, working two jobs. He did this for twenty-six years. This was not a very desirable neighborhood to raise children—many unwed mothers, parents who let their children simply run wild and not take care of their personal hygiene. It was a tough area, and as a very Christ centered household, my mother simply was frustrated at having to live and succumb to the bleak conditions that defined our neighborhood.

As a result of her discomfort, she would often fly into rages that she took out on us. My sister is nineteen months older than I and was much more capable of feigning comfort than I. Keeping us contained inside, and with no way to escape created a layer of depression and a tremendous need to feel free. I was very inclined to go along with the antics of a classmate that was friendly and prone to attempting to get their approval and attention.

The gentrification of Harlem was most notable by the many chain stores and restaurants that almost take over 125th street, home to the infamous Apollo Theater, Target, Best Buy, and KFC. They accompany the remodeled brownstones, which were residences to many of our precious cultural geniuses. The homes of Thelonious Monk, Dizzy Gillespie, Billie Holiday, Duke Ellington, and even Barrack Obama, who resided briefly in the area before establishing his residency at Columbia University, were pointed out on the tour.

Over the years, my mother, aunt, and her husband, and I would visit my uncle's apartment on the Upper West Side of Manhattan. My mother and I would fly in from Seattle before I moved to New York. My aunt and her husband would drive in from Queens.

It was reported that he was hit by a bicycle, when on a walk, and died of his injuries. I had no contact with any of his friends, and my mother and her sister were indifferent to the circumstances. This was not uncommon behavior on the part of my family and was deeply disturbing to me.

At this present moment in history, each of these individuals is deceased. A mountain of emotion and anxiety arises inside me when thinking of these relationships. My returning to his old neighborhood after twenty years was like the equivalent of placing flowers on one's grave. The very nature of those tumultuous family relationships never ceased. I desperately wanted them to. I loved my Uncle deeply, he was a very talented, outspoken, and self-defined man, always delightfully engaging me with his New

York stories. When living in New York City and attending college, I would meet my Uncle on 14th street at a fabric store known for its large array of fabrics and other sewing accessories. A loner, and very self-reliant man, he led a life solely committed to making beautiful draperies and upholstering for his clients. He was well known in his Upper West Side neighborhood for finding furniture that had been set out the street to be disposed and refinishing it.

His workshop was in the basement of his building, and I remember carving my initials on a wood board he had posted on the wall where he kept messages from clients. My mother requested him to make draperies for our living room, and she sent him the measurements. Some months later we received them, and when hung, they were made to the precise specifications and were a perfect fit for the large windows. The sewing skill is one that my mother and both of her brothers had, and we never knew where they got it.

♛

My mother took tailoring training at Seattle Central in the mid-sixties and was immediately hired at Frederick & Nelson's, an exquisite department store in downtown Seattle. She worked in alterations for sixteen years. She was able to change her status from a maid/domestic to that of someone with a job that she loved and was good at. For this reason, I hoped that she would appreciate my desire to leave Seattle for education, work, and adventure. But this was not the case. I prepared myself for my escape by taking business classes at Seattle Central in the mid- seventies; finally, I made my escape. I was told years later that she would go in my room and cry. She was tremendously attached to me. She had no relatives in Seattle, unlike my father. They left the South during the Great Migration era but did not meet until arriving in Seattle.

I loved all of them, but their memories never ceased to keep me filled with deep anxiety – the kind that is dark and brooding. They did not really care for each other, which even after death, one wonders what actions or slight could prevent a brother or sister from visiting their grave—or even knowing or caring where that sibling was buried. Nothing could be more different from this community than my old neighborhoods in Seattle.

The vast differences between the two communities serve to mirror how those differences impacted my life, my ambitions, and my tremendous need to be free from this setting.

Individuality, self-expression, attending college, to advance oneself was not encouraged in my "home." The differences in these two settings, Seattle and New York City, connected to the deepest regions in my mind-soul-spirit and created a strong need to be free from harsh judgement and indifference. It was more furious than any hurricane, tornado, or volcano that had ever found its way to any known geographical region.

"Can you stop for a moment when we reach 103rd and Manhattan Avenue?" I asked the driver. He was a beautiful Indian gentleman, and he seemed to understand my request. We would quickly approach our destination—an address that I have seen written in the upper left-hand corner on envelopes, whose insides contained letters to my mother. I well remember her receiving several while I resided at home. I anticipated his Seattle visits. It was beyond humorous to witness a conversation with my father and uncles about how to pick one of the vegetables from my father's garden. This East Coast urban dweller was preparing to unearth the vegetable from the root—separating the entire specimen from its core. As we got closer to my uncle's apartment, I could feel tears forming in my eyes, and my heart racing.

When I was seventeen years old, my mother treated me to a trip to North Carolina, New York, Pennsylvania, and Washington DC. The pride I felt when sitting in on a class with a cousin who attended Howard University was overwhelming. It was the mid-sixties, and the Black Liberation and Pan African Movement were at its peak. I was a serious Pacific Northwest student who was, in no small measure, extraordinarily impressed by these self-assured and intelligent Howard University students. Anticipating our visit, my New York uncles took me on subway rides, a play in Greenwich Village, as well as a tour of Striver's Row in Harlem, pointing out all the amazing homes of New York's highly successful Blacks. My Uncle Charles, a highly individualistic and self-defined artist, lived modestly in his studio on 103rd and Manhattan Avenue, for over fifty years. He had an excellent reputation for his work, he reported that Madam C.J. Walker was one of his clients.

Young black intellectuals at the time strongly emphasized the need to learn, to embrace Black empowerment thinking –casting off the notions of the more genteel "turn the other cheek" philosophy. Learning about one's history and regality were blasted in signing, in speeches, and in the proud presence of the all black college marching bands in Washington DC.

Nothing prepared me for what I found when descended from the taxi. *Is my uncle's apartment intact?* Would I recognize it after so many years? All I knew was that I was now ready. It was a short taxi ride, for I was staying on 93rd & Amsterdam Avenue, only a fifteen-minute drive from that infamous address: 103rd & Manhattan Avenue.

The anxiety I experienced opened dark closets hidden in the back of my mind. Why was my family indifferent toward those who express their individuality and artistry? Am I really free of the deep-seated anger and emotional abuse? Will I finally discern how this type of abuse ties into racism, and the denigration of black people?

I reflected on how far I had come to arrive at freedom on my flight from Seattle to New York. What does it mean in terms of black female struggle, sacrifice, exhilaration, betrayal, psychological denigration by family and society at large? What would it take for me to really know or recognize freedom after so much water under the bridge?

My answer, as I pondered: to simply fall in love with oneself, and the severely wounded little girl inside. To look back with gratitude, love, and forgiveness for all the lessons provided and learned. To train and use one's God given talents in service of others. To stretch out one's hand with love and gratitude, to embrace all manners of delicious freedom.

I took a deep breath before leaving the taxi, my driver was patient and understanding. As my feet touched the ground, I looked around, and nothing even vaguely resembled his old apartment bldg. There were several newer apartments, and I could not even visually duplicate the angle the apartment sat in relationship to what I was now seeing. An old grocery store that I would view from his 5th floor apartment while we were sitting in his living room, having coffee and looking out, was all that was recognizable.

I began to realize, in this present moment, on the ground viewing the store how different an experience it was from twenty years ago. With all the newer brownstones on uncle Charles' block, I sadly could not find his apartment. From the window, thirty years ago while living in New York, I had absolutely no idea of the struggle I would face in the process of really getting free, whether residing in either Seattle or New York.

Turning my head, I glanced at the cab driver, and he gave me a reassuring look to not rush this moment. I had only been standing there for five minutes, but it seemed like fifteen, as the taxi meter was still running. Grief filled my spirit as I knew it would. Gradually I began to relax in the knowledge that the acquisition of freedom is a process that I fully committed myself to for numerous years. Growing into the best version of myself through the pain has meant an unwavering belief that there are light and hope beyond what I saw from that 5th floor window.

I began to sense just how far I had come by creating a space within, and for once, reveling in the fact that though my beloved uncle had passed on; along with his brothers and sisters.

His changed neighborhood served as a metaphor for just how much things change. It is through love and forgiveness and using my talents in the world that I have found a "home" and true freedom. On that day last summer, on 103rd and Manhattan Avenue, my uncle was again teaching me.

ELNAH JORDAN

Eye of the Storm

Remember when we were kids, and we could not wait to be older? As I grew into a woman, I often heard others say, "I wish I were a kid again." "No, thank you," I politely rejected. I am now a sixty-four-year-old black woman whose childhood was interrupted by sexual abuse and cruelty. Ages eight through thirteen I escaped the clutches of my brother. By sixteen I was running from friends of my parents. I will never understand how people can be heartless and have no morals. I am from a family of seven, being the second from the oldest, and big sister to three younger siblings. Somewhere I lost my dignity, voice, self-esteem, and power. I spent most of my life as the black sheep of the family. *What did I do wrong,* I often thought. There was no support, no encouragement or conversations. To stay safe, I retreated from the line of fire. It was like I wasn't part of the family. I believed I was adopted.

In my twenties, while on vacation in Seattle, my godmother came over to visit, and took me to her home. I had not seen her since I was a preteen. She told me, "It's not your fault," I was confused by her statement. She explained the reason why I was so mistreated as a child. My godmother shared, "You remind her of your birth father, a preacher, who left her for a family friend." I was only four, but I remember it very well. What she said shocked me to my core.

I recall the lady's husband bringing a letter from my sperm donor to his wife. I saw them read it together then burn it. I never saw my father again until I looked him up as an adult. His name was never spoken in her house, ever. I sang like him and looked like him, but again it wasn't any fault of mine.

Emotions came over me in a wave that turned in to a flood. I thought I would drown. First, I felt relieved that it wasn't my imagination. Shame and embarrassment followed; everyone knew of the secret, but me. After, I felt anger because of the pain I endured as a child. It took a long time to process this, and I wanted to tell my mom I knew.

No wonder I started drinking in 7th grade. My friends stashed lots of beer and wine outside, then we would sneak to the schoolyard to drink. Often, I would babysit, drink the house liquor, and replace it with water, but people eventually caught on.

At sixteen, I left home because my mother had not invested anything in my life, and I felt worthless. Never was I asked about my dreams, plans for college, or musical ambitions. Music was my comfort, but my mother constantly shut me down. I went to night school and graduated out of sheer determination, then I left for good. My mother wouldn't answer my calls, and if she did, she would hang up. I knew then, I was on my own.

Shortly after, I flew to Florida to meet up with old friends, relax, and play music. Florida was hot with the bluest waters I have ever seen. I was still too young to get a job. So instead, I played my guitar on beaches and in coffee houses. Later, I hitched to San Francisco with a band of gay women who looked out for each other. I traveled across the United States three times, but that is another story.

I got upset because I was still alone, but I was safe from men. I had accepted that there was nothing to love about me. I parted ways with them because my voice was supporting them as street musicians, but they had each other. I stopped drinking because I had to pay attention to my surroundings. I was scared to death of the world and constantly in survival mode—but I'd rather die than go home.

I sang in the Bay area at the Cannery as a street musician. It was the most money I had ever earned, and I sang until I could get a room in the Tenderloin every night. A couple of years later, I did my first musical and met a man named Ed. He was the only man I have ever trusted. I was embraced and felt loved for the first time in my life. Ed was a dancer in the first show I was hired for, portraying the great Bessie Smith at age nineteen.

He was a handsome black gay man with a big bass voice. He taught me about the stage. I had no idea what stage right or left meant or that I was even that talented. I was dressed in my first silk stockings with the seam up the back, and I begin to explore everything anew, including feeling safe.

We were close. Ed was by my side at twenty-four-years-old when I delivered my first child. Our birthdays are a day apart, and we always celebrated them together. Later he contracted AIDS and died, being one of the first in San Francisco to do so.

Feeling helpless and lost again, I started doing crack and drinking, for I had lost another family member. I didn't care anymore; therefore, I fell deep into the drug world and depression. I stopped singing, stopped caring, and swore, I would never love again. I never dreamed I would go through the same history with Anthony, my only child.

♛

Anthony started showing signs of mental illness at age sixteen. Shortly after he was diagnosed with schizophrenia. I worked around the clock with three jobs trying to make up for my sins. He ran away, quit school, and moved with a lady who had thirteen kids. I learned he had been taking my liquor to school to self-medicate. I realized history was repeating itself. I later learned the scientific term, epigenetics.

I birthed my son, knowing I would be a single mother. He was born out of date rape. I named him Anthony after my younger brother. I didn't understand I was pregnant until I was six months along, so I had him. It never crossed my mind he would follow in my footsteps.

Without knowledge, I had passed on my substance and sexual abuse to my only son. Because I was raising him by myself, I kept two jobs, so naturally, I left him with a sitter while at work. Anthony was five when he told me my friend's son had molested him. I got my gun and began the six-mile trek to kill him. He escaped by the grace of God, dear friends, and the police. I swore that this would never happen to him, but it did. This time I called the police, we went to court, and the son of my ex-friend was put away at the age of fifteen. Anthony and I went through counseling for the next two years.

As I got deeper into drugs, I moved my son back to Seattle, hoping family would help raise him. In retrospect, my family never supported me, so how could I believe they would help him? Unfortunately, Anthony was treated in the same negative manner. I found it difficult to explain their actions to him. He was only in the 3rd grade.

The stress of the move inspired old habits to resurface. Alcohol and crack cocaine became my refuge. I was what they call a functioning addict, and the alcohol got worse. Feelings of depression and isolation returned, forcing me to slip back into cycles of addiction. It seemed I was no better than before I left. Sometimes I wonder why I stopped singing. I believe music was my spiritual outlet, so I never mixed music with substance abuse. I didn't sing for fifteen years.

Anthony stopped going to school. When I dropped him off, he would leave out the back door.

Our fighting started to get physical after he turned sixteen and was diagnosed with schizophrenia. My precious son became a father at seventeen, despite his illness. Anthony continued to steal liquor and drink it at school. The last straw was he started selling crack, which motivated me to stop smoking it cold turkey. I knew we were in big trouble.

At the age of eighteen, he went to prison for being an "irritant to the community." When he was released, he tried to live with his baby's momma, but his illness along with self-medicating escalated. I didn't want my granddaughter to know him like that. Fortunately, my granddaughter's mother finished nursing school, got him on medication, and filed for disability.

I thought he was getting it together, but it was impossible with his illness. Instead, he decided to be homeless after being removed from nine group homes. He has wandered the streets for four years and is now addicted to heroin. I have sent him to rehab six times, draining my finances. The silver lining is Anthony has a payee to ensure he doesn't spend all his money on drugs.

Anthony is forty-one, mentally ill, and homeless. I can't help but to feel his troubles are my fault. I struggle with guilt every day. Now my granddaughter is showing the same signs. I believe epigenetics has claimed another member of my heart.

What does the future hold? Can we break the cycle of trauma with his daughter? Is there anything else I can do? Will I ever bring my family together? Who knows?

AISHA NEWCHURCH

Three-Seventeen

I didn't tell my mom that I was pregnant until I was five and a half months, and even then, it was forced. I was sixteen-years-old and met the father at an All City dance that was held at my high school. He was a year older, tall, cute, and "banana yellow," as I often described him. We went on two or three dates over a four-month timeframe. We had sex one time. Immediately I knew I was pregnant. He thought I was crazy, but guess who missed her period?

While out with a friend, a guy who liked her took one look at me and asked if I were pregnant. I had always been tall and skinny, but it looked like I had a basketball hidden in my shirt from a sideview. In my mind, I had to tell her, but there was a part of me that wondered why she didn't know. For months, I had hidden tampons and pads. If a total stranger saw it, why didn't she?

My mom was a single parent of five, so she was always working. I was the middle child and responsible for my two younger brothers. If I came home right after school, did my homework, made sure they did theirs, fed them, cleaned up the house, and got them to bed—everything was fine. It was only when those chores did not happen that she paid attention.

The day I told her I was pregnant, she went ballistic. She wanted to know where it happened, and who's house I had sex in. I initially lied and told her it happened at his house. But the truth was that I got pregnant at home, in her house, and that concept seemed to be the end of it all. For her, having sex in her house was extremely disrespectful, that fact fueled her decisions from that point on.

It was decided that the baby would be given up for adoption. Well, she decided. It wasn't a situation where she asked me what I wanted. It was a situation where she said what was going to happen. Hell, even if she had asked me, I didn't dare to question her demand.

I remember my son's father and his parents came to our house for the "discussion." My mom delivered the news about the adoption. It was from that point that his parents decided to adopt the baby. My mom did not agree with them. I don't know why and never asked. I do know that she got pregnant around the same age. Looking back, I believe she didn't want me to struggle as she did.

I was six months pregnant, and in an instant, my decisions had been made for me——my body, and my baby. No questions asked. It wasn't what I wanted, but in those moments, I felt like I had no say.

My mom operated in a way that if you didn't follow her rules or what she said your life would be miserable. "Oh, you didn't scrub the bottom of the toilet with a toothbrush? Then you didn't clean the bathroom. Oh, so, you didn't put the dishes away? Then you didn't clean the kitchen." If she came home from work and saw dishes in the dish drain, she would wake us up super early in the morning to put them away. I can still hear her, "And you better not be late for school."

I didn't like wearing dresses, my mom knew this. So, what did she do? She bought me skirts and blouses, and when I didn't wear them, she took them back and gave them to her friend Donna. I don't remember having a messy room, but periodically we would come home from school to find everything pulled off the hangers, out of the dresser, and off the bookshelf. She expected us to have it clean before bed. There was never any method to her madness. We never knew why and never questioned her. We just cleaned it up.

So, like always, I went with what she said. She found an agency; the lady came out, and the process was in motion. The lady was white, and her name was Paula. I came home from school one day and Paula was there. I never spoke to her without my mom present, and my mom pretty much spoke for me, "She doesn't want to keep this baby," my mom said. "She has plenty of time, and this is what's good for the baby." I sat on the couch next to my mom. Paula sat on the sofa directly across from us. I didn't say much, so she kept talking to my mom. I remember Paula saying, "Giving the baby up for adoption was one of the greatest gifts a person could give someone." She said, "I was making the best choice for the baby," all the things she was supposed to say.

I wanted to pick the parents. Paula said she could bring books for me to look through. After she asked, "Are you sure this is what you want to do?" "Yes, it is," I lied. I don't know if she knew I was lying or that something wasn't right. I don't even know if she cared. She never asked me that question again

After gathering information, she dropped off the books the following week. "You have a little bit of time, no rush. I'll answer whatever questions I can," she offered. I immediately disconnected myself from all things baby related. I was disgusted by all the things a woman or mother would enjoy during her pregnancy.

I remember I would slap my stomach whenever it moved. Because I wasn't keeping the baby, I felt like I wasn't supposed to enjoy anything about being pregnant. Enjoying any part of it would make giving it up even harder. And so, this precious little baby suddenly became a two-year-old being scolded at the grocery store for standing in the cart.

♛

I craved pancakes. I ate them for breakfast, lunch, and dinner. I made them as soon as I got home from school so the smell would be gone before my mom got home from work, but she always seemed to know. I got in trouble for eating breakfast food when it wasn't breakfast, so I stopped eating them. My mom was a single parent of five, therefore, food needed to last. It was either that, or this was just another way for her to punish me for getting pregnant, by exerting control.

I never got a pass for being pregnant. I couldn't miss or be late for school because I wasn't feeling well. I couldn't be tired, neglect my chores, or complain that my back hurt, there was no excuse.

The baby was due January 10, 1994, one week after my seventeenth birthday. I stopped responding to Paula. I was supposed to pick the parents; instead, I ignored her calls. She was trying to bring me the books to look through, but I couldn't do it. I didn't want to do it. Three weeks before my due date, I decided to keep him. I told my mom, and I remember her not saying much besides, "Okay."

I had been working at McDonald's since I was three months pregnant. I used my own money to buy things for my son. Soon after, my mom decided that I needed to pay rent. She said, "I owed her for living with her," I didn't understand. I was a seventeen-year-old student, working part-time for a measly $5.15 an hour. I remember trying to figure out why I owed her rent. I was her child and didn't ask to come to this earth. Ultimately, I needed my mom, and I always felt like she used that to her advantage.

Her resentment toward me rendered me powerless, and she believed I would never fight back. I felt I was being punished for deciding to keep my baby. I agreed to pay her once I had all I needed for my son. WRONG ANSWER. And because it was the wrong answer, she did what she wanted and took half anyway. I didn't argue. I paid rent faithfully.

My beautiful baby boy was born at 7:06 am on January 19th. He was 6lbs, 6oz, and 21 inches long. Looking back, I had an easy labor with minimal pain. I pushed a total of four times, and he was out. To this day I get tickled thinking about his birthday. He was white as rice with straight black hair; you couldn't tell me he wasn't the cutest little thing— long but so little at the same time. I remember the hardest part of the labor was his shoulders.

I had a birthing suite, and if I remember correctly, there were only a few women having babies at that time. It was my mom and me in the room; my older sister stayed in the waiting room but came in after. I was not allowed to call the father, mama's orders. I'm not even sure he would've even come, but he never had that choice.

Before I was ready to push, the nurse asked if I'd decided on an epidural. Someone said no, but it wasn't me. I remember her saying, "She doesn't need any drugs." The nurse looked at me, looked at my mom, and then moved to the other side of the room. I didn't need the drugs, but it would have been nice to know someone had my back.

My sister came into the room to see my baby, and our mom dropped the biggest bomb. When the nurse asked if I picked out a name, my mom announced that she wanted to name my son. I'm not sure when it was decided, but it was decided. She named him, Tavares Cheyenne.

When I got to my permanent room, I thanked the Lord for giving me a small baby, locked the door, and took a long shower. It was a hard transition when I got home from the hospital. I had a baby to take care of. The same baby I had not connected to while he was inside of me, now he was my responsibility. I had decided to keep him about a week or two before I had him, so I did not have much time to retrain my brain. It felt like I was babysitting someone else's child.

It took a month for my maternal instincts to kick in. But once I found my 'mommy mode' I was good. Just before my eighteenth birthday, my mom and I had an argument. It was during a get together she and her friends were having. I don't recall exactly what was said, but she said something crazy to me in front of her friends. I felt embarrassed and disrespected, and I believe she wanted me to feel that way.

By this point, I felt I deserved more respect than she was dishing out. I was working, in school, taking care of myself, a baby, AND paying rent. I was not afraid to tell her how I felt. There had been one other time we'd gotten into it. I guess in her mind, this was strike number two. My mom kicked me out just before my eighteenth birthday, but not before she collected the rent. The first thing I took when I left that house was my son.

I describe myself as a very caring, loving, diligent responsible, and protective parent. When Nick was in preschool, I had another baby. I involved him as much as I could, so he went to doctor appointments, helped shop, and helped pack the diaper bag. His major duty as a big brother was to carry the diaper bag when we went out. I remember he looked so disappointed when we found out the baby was a boy. He had made it very clear that he wanted a sister, so the initial frown in that little room was priceless.

    I did popcorn Fridays every week, went to all the parent-teacher conferences, school carnivals, and faithfully had classroom birthday parties. My name came up on the Section 8 list right on time. I used the opportunity to go to school. It also allowed me to have more time with my boys. I still have Nick's bowling pin souvenir, the wooden clock we painted together, and the ceramic bowl he made with my name carved into it. For a long time, I had one of his tiny little diapers hidden away in a box.

    I made creative treats for various holidays: popcorn balls for Halloween with brown, orange and yellow Reese's pieces in them; heart-shaped cookies and cakes for Valentine's Day, and Easter baskets made from themed tumblers. Movie nights with all my nieces and nephews were complete with a concession stand at "intermission." I was very intentional about wanting to create very different experiences than I had when I was younger.

    I remember my mom used to pick one day to take off and spend with each of us separately. As a single parent of five, this was huge, and while I have a deep appreciation for the intent, I committed to doing more.

My work hours were flexible while Nick was in middle school. He played basketball, so attending his games was a priority, especially since his dad was not present. Nick's dad went into the Army when he was two, to say he wasn't there is an understatement. The Army allowed him to physically be absent, but I think it also made it easier to be emotionally absent. We both were young, and there was no real emotional attachment when I was pregnant.

His dad had three marriages and three other children who got to spend time with him, my son felt jaded by this fact. I pushed for them to have a better relationship, but it was easy for his dad to disconnect. My son took it personally. It was always important for me to show up; I never wanted to fit into that "single mom" stereotype. He had birthday parties every year until he turned twelve. He never got in trouble, got good grades, had positive friends, and good manners; he was an all-around respectable young man.

Nick's behavior started to change when he was twelve. He came home with his hand busted up and told me he punched a wooden post in an apartment parking lot. I don't recall what it was about, but I recall it being the first time I felt there was something brewing. I cleaned and bandaged his hand and attempted to have the first of many conversations about anger.

In 2009, we moved to South Carolina. I liked the state, and the woman I was dating was from there. I wanted to get my master's degree, and her family agreed to help us if we moved. The idea of having support while in school was attractive. I saw it as a win-win situation, so we moved.

Nick's dad lived near us; therefore, he got to spend time with him; however, this is when the shit hit the fan. He did more damage than good. Nick's dad was not a good father to my son. It seemed he allowed his wives to take on more of a parental presence in my son's life than I felt was needed. It was frustrating to hear school shopping could not happen unless the wife were with them. This made no sense to me.

I don't have a clue what the actual truth was, but I never received a dime from them. Needless to say, this created more issues for my son. He had long felt that his dad put other people before him. He was hurt, but he wasn't talking to me about his feelings. Out of worry, I put him in counseling.

We moved back to Washington two years later. My relationship ended, and it was best to come back. We had no family there and zero support. In my mind, I wanted to put him back in his comfort zone, so we returned to our old neighborhood. I was in my last month of grad school. I arranged for my sons to stay with a good friend, so I could stay in South Carolina and finish school. I had a house sale every weekend. I let folks walk through and buy whatever they wanted. I left that place with some clothes, my computer, a couple of totes of irreplaceable items, and my dog. It took me several years to piece together everything I'd lost mentally, physically, and emotionally. The entire drive was a blur. I just know I made it back in three days, from a drive that should've taken five. As soon as I crossed the Washington State border, my body immediately let out one of the most productive cries I've ever experienced. I was home.

We bounced around from different friend's houses for four months. I woke at five a.m. to get them to school and then to find a Park and Ride to sleep before going to work. I hoped and prayed every single time that no one called the police on me. It was a struggle.

I started work about two weeks after I got back. No time to adjust. No time to process. I was in survival mode. I had two boys to look after. I didn't know if I was coming or going half the time, but our needs were getting met. There was no furniture in our first apartment, but it was ours. The first piece of furniture that I purchased was bunk beds.

Nick finished high school early. Prom wasn't ideal, but I made the best of it within my means. I offered to fully support him if he went to college. He went for maybe one week. He decided he was grown at seventeen—tattoos, ear piercings and coming home when he felt like it followed.

Nick worked part-time, however, at some point, he started doing other stuff to make money. I found out when King County Sheriffs arrived at my house. My son owed some dude money, and the dude came to collect. I was thankful there were no weapons involved. This was my last straw. I refused to let his younger brother watch him disrespect to me. I asked Nick to leave my house. I was not okay with his behavior and the traffic he attracted to our home. A major concern was the dude could come to my house with a gun. The last time I checked; bullets have no name attached to them. I imagined us opening the door and catching one or two of those nameless bullets.

I loathed asking him to leave. It felt eerily like the conversation I had with my mom at his age. My mom accused me of being disrespectful to her also. It took a moment to realize that although the circumstances were similar, how I'd arrived at my decision was gravely different. I asked my son to find five of his black friends whose single moms were willing to fully support them if they went to college. I don't think he ever found them; and if he did, he never brought them to me.

Since Nick moved out, our relationship has been extremely rocky. He argues when I offer my advice or opinion. His friends will co-sign the crazy things he comes up with, but as his mom, I will not do it. I did not think it was okay to enroll in a $50k degree program when he could qualify for grants. I've had to learn to let go and let him live his life. I wanted to do better than my mom. I never want my sons to question my love or actions toward them. It is important that they know I have their backs. Lastly, I hope they know that they can trust me as a person, mother, and woman.

Everyone in my life understands the unwavering dedication I have for my sons. When I reflect on my life and my parenting, I can't recall a time I have wronged them or favored one over the other. I've never let anyone abuse or talk crazy to them. I've considered them with every decision I've made.

Like most parents, I've made decisions in the moment, but I don't regret a thing. And, like most single black moms, I busted my tail to make things happen. So, imagine my reaction when I became the reason for all things wrong in Nick's life. It hurt me to my core to have this child of mine, that I had dedicated my entire life to, dump all his weight on me. I knew better; however, there were parts of me that felt responsible for the shortcomings he'd experienced.

I backtracked all the choices I have made. All the people I introduced into our spaces. Each person I removed from our life. The love, warmth, and limitless times I soothed this troubled heart. I never questioned the validity of his feelings, but I did question the validity of his perspective.

Over the years, I've thought about the continuation of generational cycles and how they surface when you least expect them. My mom had a rocky relationship with her mother. She and I had a tumultuous bond, and now, there is Nick and me. I never hurt Nick on purpose. I never intentionally gave him bad advice.

Most importantly, I never cheated him or stole from him. He's never been a "bitch," "slut," or "punk." There was never a single time that I reduced him to how I felt about his dad. I've always treated him like a person and allowed him to make his own decisions, even if I did not agree.

I often wonder about the disconnect when I was pregnant. It was such a small fraction of time, but I sometimes question the impact it had on our relationship. After examining and reexamining my life, I don't see my fault. Sure, I wasn't perfect, but I am not responsible for his decisions.

I don't have a favorite child; I treat my children equally. I loved, cared for, and provided for both effortlessly. Nick is twenty-five now and I owe him nothing but unconditional love, and (boundary ridden) support. It took me some time to get here, but I made it without any regrets. My choices were my own, and I can live with them all. The relationship that I had with my mom existed as a result of her childhood experiences. Although her experiences had nothing to do with me, they inevitably became mine and my sons.

March 17, 2017, my mother passed away unexpectedly. Whatever the seventeen-year-old girl within needed from her disappeared just as quickly as she took her last breath. I sat in the room, next to her, until the funeral home came to remove her body. I cried to her, prayed for her, and most importantly, I forgave her. She had done her best, and I was okay with accepting that. I just hope it doesn't take my baby as long to forgive me.

NATALIA PIERSON

Claiming my Magic

"Natalia is a white girl's name," said one of my two black female professors on the first day of Social Work class. Although it often gets confused for Natalie and I can never find a key chain at any gift shop, I love my name. My name is unique. I occasionally have the joy of confusing new clients when they see me with kinky corkscrew hair and café au lait mixed skin, not the Russian woman they were expecting. I mostly love my name because it was a great name for elementary school. Natalia is almost impossible to turn into a stupid nickname. It wasn't until middle school that I found kids determined enough to create a nickname that encapsulated that I was a white girl in a black body.

My hair, like the head that wore her, does not like being told what to do. My hair has a mind of her own. When I was young, no one helped me foster a relationship with her. My black dad was often at work or on deployment and never taught me to deal with textured hair. Either way, I wouldn't have asked because he always hurt my head when he tried the simplest braid. So that left my white mom to deal with the mess that was my hair. Although she earned a cosmetology license, her bone straight thin brown hair gave her no experience with my strong-willed black curls. She had always threatened to cut off my hair if I didn't take care of it. I was afraid of a short fro because I thought it would make me look blacker.

I was a confused biracial girl. I didn't want to look blacker than I already did. From school and society, I knew to get anywhere, I needed to be as white as possible. With my dad away, I was raised in the white culture. My mother and her family, and many of my peers welcomed me into their white folds. Although, being in Southern California and among fellow Navy brats exposed me to a broad scope of diversity. My skin tone could let me pass for some other nondescript minority, but my hair yells, "We got a black girl here!"

I tried to relax my hair and remove the clear marker of my blackness, but I never had the beautiful straight hair promised to me on the box. I have never learned how to get my frizzy hair to obey the heat and lie down. Instead, I had a bird's nest on my head that I just tied up in a bun, like a disobedient child in time out.

In the middle of 7th grade, my dad got reassigned. My family moved from the only home I knew to Southern Maryland, about an hour south of DC. I hated the move, and I hated that place. I missed the ocean breeze and the sound of seagulls. I hated leaving my friends in the middle of 7th grade to move to a new school. I hated the impossible task of making new friends. I didn't want to meet new people. I wanted to go back home.

Most of all, I hated the melanin version of the Mean Girls. These girls stood together on the outskirts of the crowd. They all had beautiful skin in a variety and the fierceness that only black girls possess. Because I didn't own that, I was an easy target. Like a limping gazelle, the lionesses pounced at the easy kill. They took every opportunity to make fun of everything that made me different. I didn't talk like them or understand their slang. I didn't know what a cornrow was or how to make my hair sheen like theirs. Instead of inviting me into the sisterhood, they kicked my ass out with a bitch slap when one of them created the name "Nappyalia."

My nappy and frizzy hair broadcasted to the world that I have no fucking clue how to live in my skin. It's ridiculous that I've allowed these teen girls this much power over my self-worth as a woman of color. I can't even remember their names. What I remember is their scornful laughter and glee of finding the name that pegs me as the fraudulent black girl. They stripped me of the ability to identify as a black woman with confidence. They knew I didn't belong. It's like they saw discomfort in my body and aimed their missiles straight at it. In the wilds of middle school hierarchy, if they could take me down a peg, they could take a higher place on the social ladder.

Cognitive dissonance let me believe that the world saw us as equals on the same playing field. All the while, I knew that I was better than them because they were mean, angry, and dangerous black girls. Perhaps it was because of my lighter skin, my white mother, and "good hair" I didn't know what to do with.

Maybe I knew I was better than them because I didn't have to fight as hard to be labeled as smart and capable. Perhaps we were picking up the weapons left from ancestors who battled the superiority of being in the big house or the field, all the while forgetting that we both were wearing shackles.

We all bought into the lie that success can only be achieved on the back of other women, particularly other women of color. I am done with handing over my power to nameless girls who were also struggling to find their own place in this rigged world. I am tired of feeling that I don't belong in spaces where I can finally exhale and blend in with beautiful variations of skin tone and hairstyles that mirror my own. The whispers of my ghosts will no longer validate my blackness. I will do blackness my own mosaic way. I won't seek permission to be me in the world.

Misguided teenage girls will no longer be my guidebook for blackness. My beautiful hair with a mind of her own, the broad nose of my father, my smooth brown skin, and my thick thighs are all that I need to tap into my own black girl magic. My black girl magic has sprinkles of white, black, and grey.

My magic includes the determination of my grandfather to be a landowner away from the city. My magic includes the strength of my granny who never had trees by her home because if a mob was going to lynch her or her family, she wasn't going to make it easy for them. And yes, my magic has some skeletons of enslavers. We all carry this legacy in our flesh and bones. We are all responsible for healing our sisterhood. Who else, but us, will shut down the lies, and proclaim that black is beautiful? Black is not a minority, black is power, and black is enough.

NAHNI GIBSON

Our Journey is One

I grew up in a broken home, raising my sister at the age of eight. My mother was absent for the most part, she was a mixture between an alcoholic and a workaholic. She spent very little time with us, and seldomly showed affection. One thing we knew for sure was that our mom knew how to provide, but that's all she knew how to do. We knew if she had a bad day, the house better be clean, or we better stay out of her way. Whenever my mom felt like she couldn't deal with me, she would threaten to kick me out. She started making threats when I was around twelve-years-old. When I was fourteen, she finally made good on her word. I was told to leave and never come back. I grew tired of hearing that same sentence countless times, so I did exactly what she said, I left.

I remember how cold and dark it was outside. I couldn't take anything with me except the clothes on my back. It was the middle of the night. I had on Eeyore pajama pants and a tank top. No jacket, socks, or shoes. It was raining, the cold, wet ground pierced the bottoms of my feet. But I kept moving until I arrived at my friend's house. She wasn't home, so I ran a little further to my next friend's home, luckily, she was there. I called my dad to come and get me, but my mom told him if he came anywhere near me, she would call the police.

The relationship with my mother stopped there until I was about eighteen. I'd matured enough to appreciate my mother, but I resented her for failing to teach me how to be a woman. Lost, confused, and all alone, I entered the cold world. I grew close to a woman named Heather, who dated my dad. She grew up in the streets; therefore, she taught me everything I needed to know about surviving.

As I got older, I realized I was stuck in the same cycle. I didn't love myself or others, I had no confidence, and my idea of being strong was backwards. I believed strength meant showing no emotion and not letting anyone in. For me, being strong gave me control of all things. I walked through life, unaware of my worth. I grew to understand my happiness, and reality is mine to create. I didn't know the only way to retain peace was by refusing to allow another person to take it from me. I learned all of this during the most traumatic experience of my life.

Although I grew up in the streets, I still had plans for myself. I continued going to school. When I turned sixteen, I got my first job, then I graduated high school. Shortly after I began college, I found out I was pregnant, but I pushed through. If I learned anything from my mom, it was how to provide, but I didn't want to be the same type of parent. I wanted my son to know he's handsome, worthy, smart, and capable of anything he puts his mind to. Most importantly, I needed him to know how much his mommy loves him.

♛

October 14, 2014, I met my handsome son, Xavier Rashad. He was perfect, sweet kissable chubby cheeks, soft sun kissed skin, big beautiful deep brown eyes, and silky-smooth black hair. I held him tightly and ran my lips along the top of his head. I didn't want to let him go. I watched him grow into an intelligent, kind, and loving little boy. But on November 24, 2017, my whole world was flipped upside down.

Xavier had been sick for a few days. I had taken him to three different hospitals, and they all told me the same thing. Finally, I took him to Seattle Children's Urgent care. He was immediately placed on oxygen and transported to the hospital via ambulance. It was a downward spiral from there. My son, who had just turned three a month prior, was close to death.

My baby was so sick he was intubated and put on life support. For seventy days, I couldn't hear Xavier's voice or see his perfect smile. To make matters worse, he couldn't breathe on his own. They told me he wouldn't make it. I was harboring so much pain, pretending I'm in control because, through all of this, I still needed to be strong for my youngest child.

My daughter was two-months-old at the time. I was put in a position where I had to choose and prepare. Choose which child needed me more, my dying son, or my newborn. I was told I had to prepare for the death of my first child who hadn't had a chance to fully live.

My faith was self-taught, but I prayed. I prayed so much my knees were black and blue. On February 10th, Xavier was taken off life support and could breathe on his own. Suddenly, I didn't feel so helpless and angry at the world. But that was short lived, our journey had only just begun.

One day, while Xavier and I played, he started to destat, his lung had collapsed. I was rushed out of the room, and consent forms were shoved in my face. "I don't care what you have to do, just take care of my baby," I roared. Petrified, my feet wouldn't move. They told me I couldn't stand outside his room. I refused to leave, "That's my son," I wailed. It felt like hours had gone by. Finally, I was let back in. Four bilateral chest tubes were placed between his tiny ribs to decompress the air leaking from his lungs. Again, the doctors told me he wouldn't make it, but I refused to believe. My mother never gave me to tools to process the pain I felt. Repeatedly, I was told that my son's illness was my fault. I was all alone, except for my babies.

The father of my children didn't want us in his home, so I took the baby and left. I moved our stuff into Xavier's room, where we lived for four months. I was so confused, never have I felt so much pain. I found myself constantly in the unknown, but I had to keep my faith.

A few weeks later, things began to look up. The doctors tell me there's a chance we can save his life. Without a doubt, I agreed to a tracheostomy. His surgery was scheduled for the end of March. We did our best to prepare him for the procedure. The surgeons introduced themselves, each of them had a little toy or something for Xavier. We asked him if he is ready, and he nods. As they pushed his bed out of the room, I kiss him and assure him everything is going to be okay.

The surgery was successful, and I could finally see my baby's face, but again, I was petrified. I watched the team of doctors, nurses, and surgeons push my son's bed into place. I've never been so scared and excited at the same time. Finally, I could see his sweet face, and after a little therapy, hear his voice. Though happy, all I could focus on was the clench I felt in my heart and the smell of the disinfectant they used in the operating room.

The doctors were eager to give updates and talk about next steps. Eventually, I gained enough strength to walk over to his bed and look at him. I grabbed his little hand and rubbed it with my thumb, he was still out cold because of the anesthesia. He looked so perfect and comfortable.

Just before his surgery, I was blessed with an opportunity to work with a local nonprofit organization named Powerful Voices. I found an apartment the month after. I always reflect on the people and the advice I received during our stay at Seattle Children's Hospital. One thing that stuck was a nurse who told me, "Focus on the things you can control, not the things you can't control."

Xavier spent six months in the ICU and a total of eleven months in the hospital. I'll never forget the lessons I learned. During the hardest time of my life, I learned how to accept the things I can't change. I learned how to set boundaries and be transparent without fear. I also learned how to forgive and love openly.

Xavier's tender heart and bravery made an impact on everyone. When he left the hospital room, everyone was in awe. All the doctors and nurses lined up along the hall. We formed a tunnel, cheered, and showered him with bubbles as he sat in the wheelchair. "Your son is proof that doctors don't know everything," a kind physician shared.

We moved on to rehab, he learned to walk and gain strength and mobility in his hands. He was able to talk and play, and finally, my ears were blessed with the words I never thought I'd hear him say, "I love you, mommy." It was music to my ears. I held him tight and cried.

Life support, kidney failure, and some new gear, regardless of the circumstances my SON IS STILL HERE! I went through so many emotions during these times. I came to realize that the strength I needed wasn't something anyone could have taught me. Xavier's brush with death taught me how to be strong.

It was October 14th, and Xavier was four. My little warrior had conquered every battle fate had in store. We had a discharge date of October 30, 2018. My son would finally come home and make our family whole. I had been working so hard to prepare for that day.

As the months went by, Xavier continued to grow stronger. He runs and plays with his baby sister like they never missed a moment. Their relationship is inspirational. Xavier has been home five months now, and we continue to receive good news. Having a kidney transplant has been on our radar for quite some time. Recently, we had our first meeting with the transplant team at Seattle Children's. Although I decided to go with a living donor, he's still been placed on a list for a kidney.

For the next three to six months, Xavier will prepare for his transplant. Once he's finished, we can start looking for a donor, and he will have a new kidney. When he gets his transplant, there will be many things to look forward to.

He still has a ventilator because dialysis puts pressure on his lungs and makes it hard for him to breathe. The Pulmonologists says he's doing great. His lungs are healing well, and we have talked about decannulation after his transplant. There will be no more dialysis and no more ventilator.

I feel my strength comes from my son, and my light comes from my daughter. This experience forced me to grow in ways I didn't know I could grow. My biggest growth came from learning forgiveness and unconditional love. I no longer have anger and resentment for those who hurt me.

My strength, after everything he has been through, remains the most tender-hearted boy I have ever met. He is so compassionate and understanding. He knows exactly who he is, where he's been, and where he is going. At four-years-old, it seems as though he has it all figured out. He is my inspiration.

Many people say my light came at a bad time, but I believe she came at the perfect time. The hospital had brightly colored walls. I recall walking down those halls with my baby in my arms. She put a smile on everyone's face and kept my heart full. She is my motivation. Our journey will continue even after his transplant, but I know as long as I have my strength, inspiration, and motivation; everything will fall into place.

SALMA SALEH

Collateral Lessons

My father wasn't a big man in size or stature. You would rarely find him in casual wear. He always liked to dress up no matter the occasion. Both of his parents passed away when he was young, so his oldest sister raised him. Which I think is the reason why he tends to have a more sensitive side. I grew up very close to my father. When I moved away to University, I had a hard time living apart from my family. He immediately sensed that. He called me every day for months to catch me up on everything that was happening at home. He briefed me on my younger sisters' shenanigans to help me feel connected and supported. I would look forward to these phone calls every night.

Growing up, family friends filled our house constantly. My dad was charming and could socialize with just about anyone. Even my friends loved to sit and chat with him when they came over. Everyone loved the energy he would bring into the room. He was generous, eager to help anyone in need. We would occasionally have family friends staying at our house because they had come on bad times and my father wanted to help. I was annoyed to have to share our small space at the time, but now, I look at those memories with fondness.

Over the years, my father has changed. I think, as he is getting older, he is reflecting on his life and realizing there are things he wishes were different. A few summers ago, my sisters and I got into an intense argument with him. I was at my parent's house for dinner that night. It was a warm evening in June, the house smelled of cumin and coriander from the delicious meal my mother cooked.

The house was vibrant, as it usually is when everyone is home. I have a big family; there are eight of us in total. I have two brothers and three sisters, so it can sometimes feel like a bazaar—people bustling every which way. The girls in my family are social, loud, and are typically deemed obnoxious by the boys. The boys are quiet and more reserved. We are all pretty laid back, protective of each other, and for the most part, all get along well.

After dinner, we usually sit in the family room together, drinking tea and rehashing old stories. We discuss politics, Egyptian culture, or which of our friends in the community we can introduce to my older brother. My parents were convinced that he would not meet anyone without intervention.

That night, the women got up to clear the table, as is typical in my family, while the men stood around, pretending to be busy, giving off an illusion of benevolence. The argument started right before we finished up with dinner so my brothers, to avoid confrontation, snuck upstairs.

My father started the conversation by berating us for not praying and practicing Islam the way our cousins did back in Egypt. As a thirty-year-old woman who believes that your devotion to faith and religious practice is personal and private, I was already worked up. I was puzzled that he would even compare us to our cousins who were born and raised in a predominantly Muslim country.

We spent the greater part of that evening trying to defend ourselves. My dad told us, in no uncertain terms, that he wished we turned out differently. I could see the hurt and anger in my sisters' eyes. I recognized it because I felt the same way.

My parents got married young. They were in their early twenties when I was born. Shortly after I turned four years old, they decided to move to America, away from their family and friends. Far away from traditions, customs, and religion.

Growing up in America, my parents were concerned about culture. They knew we could not afford to consistently travel back home, so they connected with a few Egyptian families to start an Egyptian Cultural Association. They wanted to keep us as connected to our culture as possible. My parents made sure we celebrated cultural events together, but religion was never prioritized, it was more of an afterthought. These events were infrequent and did not demand the level of commitment required to nourish a strong religious connection.

I know my parents were busy while we were young. They worked multiple jobs to make ends meet. My parents, each with a university education in tow, struggled to find work when we first moved to America.

My late grandfather owned a business in Egypt that provided medicine and other supplies to medical institutions, but that was never enough for my father. He did not want an inherited empire; he wanted to build his own legacy. He had big dreams, but when he arrived in America, the land of opportunity, he was surprised to discover, that this was going to be much harder than he anticipated.

After completing a post-graduate certificate program, he embarked on his first venture. He started a consulting practice helping newcomers navigate the American system and providing them with the tools to succeed. The organization was prosperous and received much praise for filling a gap for the Egyptian community. My parents used the money they saved to buy our first home.

Throughout the years, the American government took a hard position on immigration; reducing the number of immigrants every year. This made working in this field complicated. My dad decided to move the family back to Egypt to take his position, give my siblings a much-needed refresher on culture, and the Arabic language.

Everyone moved except my brother and me as we were in University at the time. While he was there, he attempted to start many businesses, but nothing took off. My family spent about five years in Egypt, and my father returned more frustrated and hungrier to make a name for himself.

When they moved back, I immediately noticed the change. It had been a long time since we all lived in the same house together. I realized my father became agitated easily; the slightest thing would set him off. Anytime anyone tried to offer an alternate opinion, it would be perceived as disrespect, which would enrage him further. He could not be reasoned with.

As a child, you think your parents are perfect, and they have all the answers. It was all too clear that my father was just as lost as the rest of us. He felt inadequate and unsuccessful, like he was not enough. Enough for what? I will never understand. He started to surround himself with people he felt emulated "success." Almost as if being "successful" adjacent would make him feel better about himself, but it seemed to have the opposite effect.

He constantly measured himself up against all these individuals. Not realizing that this exercise would never lead to peace and fulfillment. There will always be someone more successful, more accomplished, and wealthier than you are. I want to do something, but I feel paralyzed. I want to tell him that he is enough, but I do not know how. I have no frame of reference for what that conversation would even look like.

I realize now that our argument about religion that night had nothing to do with religion after all. It had nothing to do with my siblings and me. It was my father yet again, feeling small because someone had something he did not. Feeling as if he was not enough because his brother had raised more religious kids than him.

As I think about starting a family, I want to do many things differently. I want my children, if God blesses me, to feel like they are enough, always. To never measure themselves up against others. To constantly want to develop and grow but for themselves, not for anyone else. Not for me, not for their father, not for the community, for themselves.

I want them to learn that happiness and fulfillment come from within. I want my children to get into the habit of checking in with themselves and checking in with us. I want my precious babies to recognize that they feel emotions, to learn to identify them and break destructive cycles. I want to empower them with all the tools to be introspective, strong, and in control. I just hope I learn how to do it first.

FONCI RICHARDSON

My Rose in Bloom

I wanted to have a family like the Huxtables. I just knew I would be married and have three kids, by the same father, of course. I figured life wouldn't be perfect but if we were together that was all that mattered. Everything changed when Calvin, my daughter's dad, told me, "If you have that baby, I'll never speak to you again." My heart sank so deep in my chest that I was numb. I thought, how could he say that? He said he loved me. I couldn't speak but, in my mind, I said, *Fuck him! Who was he to give me an ultimatum? I don't need him; we'll be fine without him.*

As the months passed, my stomach grew bigger. I remember having bouts of happiness and reading books on "What to expect when you're expecting." I carried these books like they were my bible clinging onto every word. My mother never spoke to me about the "birds and the bees," pregnancy or anything. I was nervous, curious, and excited.

I wanted to know about the changes that would alter my body over the next few months. I tried to plan my pregnancy right; I took Lamaze classes only to be disappointed by Calvin's absence. Most times he wouldn't come, so friends and family stepped in to support me. It was humiliating to be in a class full of couples, where I witnessed men supporting their women during the most crucial time of their lives.

Deep down, I was lonely. I wanted to be supported by my baby's father, but he didn't show up, and it hurt me deeply. I wanted a healthy pregnancy to reflect on. Despite his absence, I was determined to get the knowledge I needed to bring my baby into the world. Although, the thought of not knowing how my body would change, and the growth stages of the baby seemed strange.

I recall waking up that morning about 5:30 a.m. the morning of January 28th with light cramps. As the morning progressed, they seemed to be coming and going often. At first, I thought they were the

Braxton Hicks contractions I had experienced earlier in my pregnancy, but these felt different. About 10:00 a.m. I told my daughter's dad that I thought I was in labor. I told him to take me to my doctor's office to double check. Dr. Braxton told me that I was dilated and to check-in at Swedish Hospital. I was stunned, but feelings of nervousness covered me like a blanket.

"Okay, I'll check-in," I agreed. Instead, I ordered Calvin to take me home.

"You hear me?" I demanded. "Take me back home!"

Confused, Calvin responded, "What are you doing? You're supposed to check into the hospital."

"I need to go home and pack my clothes."

"I can pack them for you."

"No, I will pack them. You might forget something."

I recall Calvin shaking his head and looking puzzled. I'm sure he thought I was crazy. We lived seven minutes from Swedish. Our drive home was quiet; I was nervous and scared.

Going home was my way of stalling. I wasn't ready to face the reality of being a parent. As much reading and planning that I had done up until that point, none of it shielded me from feeling afraid. I was worried my entire pregnancy. I had gone through my pregnancy alone. Deep down, I knew it would continue that way, although I lived in the house with my daughter's dad. In short, I was cleaning, thinking, reflecting, and trying to get myself mentally prepared to walk into that hospital. I stayed in my bedroom, with the door closed, packing and making sure the room was ready for us to come home. I wanted to be alone, and the cleaning soothed my nerves.

Two hours later, I told Calvin I was ready to go. I stood in front of Swedish Hospital, took a deep breath, and walked through the sliding glass doors to check-in. Twenty-two hours later, on January 29th at 1:30 a.m., my little princess was born. Britani Rose weighed eight and a half pounds and twenty-two inches long. I was excited and exhausted at the same time. I felt like I'd been the fight of my life.

After a couple of days, we returned home with my daughter's father and life went on as usual. I stayed home and learned how to be a mother while Calvin worked. I hoped we could resume being a family. I quietly observed and watched him as time lapsed.

I felt lonely, and Calvin was dating other women. Sometimes he wouldn't come home at night. I wasn't his girlfriend, but it was hard to watch him move on. I felt disrespected by him and myself. Eventually, I decided to move home with my parents.

Two weeks later, there was a knock at my parent's door and in walked Calvin. I was surprised to see him and immediately felt something was up. Calvin visited for a while. When I turned around, Calvin got down on one knee and proposed to me. Again, I was shocked because I sure wasn't expecting that at all. I agreed, but in the back of my mind and my heart, I knew he wasn't the man for me. I accepted the ring because I didn't want to humiliate him at that moment. There was part of me that wanted to give him another chance, so, I did.

Britani and I moved back in with Calvin, again, I quietly observed, and concluded that he wasn't ready to get married. I believed his friends were telling him to do the right thing, he wanted to, but his actions displayed something different. I asked myself what would make me want to marry someone? I wanted a healthy relationship with a man that was loving, supportive, and protective. Feeling safe was important to me; I also wanted to feel cherished, valued, and content.

Until that point, I had experienced heartache and disregard. I didn't feel emotionally safe with Calvin; most importantly, I didn't trust him. I thought he hated women because he mistreated them, but he loved them when it was convenient for him. In short, I realized our relationship was unhealthy, and I knew in my heart that I had to choose my baby girl and me.

It took a couple of weeks of reflecting and toggling back and forth before I made a decision. I wanted that white picket fence, but I knew Calvin wasn't for me. I left the ring on the corner of his dresser. It remained there for two weeks, until one day, it was gone. There was no discussion about it, not even to this day. I went back because I wanted to give our relationship another try. I needed to know I had tried my best; I have no regrets. Sure, I might have stayed too long, but I felt grounded in my decision to leave. I also knew that once I made up my mind, Calvin would never have a chance at being in my life again.

I took my time because I knew there would be no turning back for me ever. I quietly started looking for a job, and about six months later, my daughter and I moved into our 1st apartment together. It was my baby girl and me against the world!

In the early stages, parenting a toddler was a challenge, but I had a beautiful little girl counting on me. As my daughter grew, I made sure she was taken care of. She had everything she needed, but it was tough being a single parent. I was her source of entertainment. I was constantly in "do" mode. It seemed my schedule circulated around my job, my daughter's school, sports, cooking, or cleaning.

It was hard, but I enjoyed watching my daughter grow up. She was always around family; never alone. My little girl was sweet, happy, funny, and smart. I planned out every day, making sure all our activities were covered. We lived our life by a (to do list) daily. It was the only way I could keep myself sane and accomplish tasks. I strived for perfection and worked tirelessly to get the list shorter, but the list kept growing.

As a single mother, I took pride in parenting my daughter. I suppose I obsessed about making sure my baby was well taken care of. All my decisions were centered around my baby girl. I was proud of the care that I had given my daughter. I believed I did a good job.

We made it through her preteens safely. In high school, Britani tells me she's pregnant. My world was crushed. I had the birds, and the bees talk with my daughter. I even asked her if she wanted to get on birth control. She said she didn't need it. I made a decision to put her on "the pill" because I wanted to ensure she was protected. At the time, my daughter had two full rides to college. I wanted my daughter to have a better life than I did. I wanted her to live out her early twenties and be free to figure herself out. I desired her to have a family with a partner who knows how to build a family.

I longed for her to have that because she came from a broken home. I thought those experiences would help steer her another way. I suppose in some ways, I shielded her from my trials and tribulations in life. My family was full of single women raising kids. I thought that was enough to make her want something different. It was hard raising a child as a young mother. To me, a woman sixteen to twenty-two is not equipped to have kids, period. I didn't want my daughter to be a statistic, another beautiful black woman struggling to raise kids on her own.

I struggled to celebrate her new reality. I was riddled with pain and guilt for allowing my daughter to go live with her boyfriend's family. I didn't know how to handle the fact that my daughter had rejected my solution to getting an abortion.

I was numb, angry, sad, and disappointed. I was afraid of the future, so I shut down emotionally and didn't know how to help my daughter. I was an emotional wreck, afraid to show my feelings to anyone. I felt if I cried, I wouldn't stop, so I kept up the appearance of being strong.

Anytime I tried to talk about it to family, they would say, "She's grown now!" I was shocked at their response. "How does having a child at seventeen make any girl grown?" I couldn't understand their way of thinking. I realized that young black woman having children out of wedlock is normal. I also came to the realization that, once again, I was alone. I was experiencing one of the lowest points in my life, and I needed some help and guidance.

I tried talking to the women in my family, but they couldn't understand my angst. I wasn't surprised. Many of them had lost sight of their own hopes and dreams long before; therefore, venting about expectations for my daughter, was a waste of time. I felt betrayed by my family, but I carried on. I became quiet and dropped communication with everyone.

I cried every morning for six months, prayed to God to release the hurt in my heart, then I ushered in acceptance. I had to make peace with my daughter and the fact that I was going to be a grandmother.

It took awhile to come out of my shell, but when I finally surfaced, I understood that I had abandoned my daughter at her darkest hour. I realized she was afraid, hurt, scared, and lonely. I had pushed her away when she needed me most.

♕

As time passed, we became distant and bumped heads often. I thought the friction between us was normal. I was told by friends that sometimes mothers and daughters have volatile relationships. In my heart, I felt there was something deeper—a deep resentment towards me, but I didn't know why. I felt animosity and bitterness. I heard the disdain in my daughter's voice when she addressed me. She treated me unkind. Some days she was a straight bitch!

Years crept by, and our relationship continued to deteriorate. Sometimes we wouldn't speak for weeks or months. Finally, after five years of back-and-forth, she agreed to counseling. I was at my breaking point and so to perserve our relationship, I kept my distance. I didn't know how to help her talk to me. It seemed anything I said was wrong. I couldn't fix the void she felt.

It was in a counseling session that my daughter turned, looked at me, and said, "I don't feel any emotional connection to you." I was in shock. Once again, my heart sank. I was numb. I knew I didn't feel the love from my daughter, and I often wondered if she even loved me. She had a lack of empathy for me but would give support to others when needed.

I've tried to be her rock, but I notice when I needed her, she didn't show up. On many occasions, I've felt like our relationship is a one way street. I believe that my daughter tolerates me because I am her mother. I've trained myself not to react and to stay cautiously optimistic.

I noticed when my daughter hugs me, it feels forced. Many times, she won't hug me before she leaves, and that hurts. She treats me like a stranger. I remember getting mad and defensive in the counseling session because I feel I gave up my life for my daughter. I sacrificed my hopes and dreams for her. To say she "felt no connection" to me, felt disrespectful. I thought about her childhood, and the time we spent together. We were like Bonney and Clyde. It was her and me all the way, so I thought.

After the counseling session, I raced home, pulled out my trunk of pictures, and started going through them one-by-one. I looked for pictures with us hugging, holding hands, and embracing. I sat in the livingroom for hours, surrounded by photos. I wanted to prove her wrong, but there wasn't a lot of us together hugging, laughing, and celebrating one another. I loved pictures and had a lot of them, but I was always the one behind the camera, which meant she was in most pictures by herself.

I remember my heart sank in my chest again. I continued to sift through memories; newborn to 7th grade, what I saw broke my heart. I felt shame for not seeing her pain. I provided for my daughter, many times with my back against the wall, all the while, fighting to keep a roof over our heads. I offered the fundamentals, but amid my struggle, I was absent. I struggled so hard, I didn't have time to cry, or feel sorry for myself.

As I reflect on my upbringing, I often wondered how my mother raised four girls who were stair stepped in age. She was a married stay at home mother who held things down effortlessly. She loved taking care of others; especially her children.

We had everything we wanted and needed. As the years went by things changed in her marriage and life. As teens we went our separate ways and I began to feel emotionally distant with my mother. I now understand that I held on to the ideal of who I wanted my mother to be, not realizing she was human. When I let go of that ideal and allowed myself to see her, I realized that my mother was everything I needed. I thank God I was able to tell her that I understood, honored, and respected her sacrifice.

Being a single parent is the hardest job in the world. I thought I had it figured out, but in my quest to provide for her needs, she suffered emotionally. During the counseling session, I apologized to Brittani for failing her as a parent. I looked her in the eyes, and I told her, "Raising you was the hardest job I've ever experienced, but I kept trying and fighting because I loved you. Please forgive me."

Since then, I've had more time to sit with my daughter and reflect on what I could have done differently. I could've held her close and told her I love her more often. I could've spent more quality time with her, so she felt my love for her despite my struggle. I understand that although we were in the home together, I was emotionally unavailable.

I can't go back and correct the mistakes I made, but as sure as I write this, understand that little girl was my breath. She was my life; she was my reason for pushing and enduring all the struggles, trials, and tribulations of being a single parent.

My advice to young mothers is to tell your children, even as you struggle, that you love them. Be available with your mind and heart. Don't be afraid to share your dreams and ambitions over dinner. Make a habit of asking your children questions and listening to their responses. Give your children eye contact and lots of physical touches because they need it. Most importantly, apologize to your kids when you mess up.

Our children don't need grand gestures to feel loved. It is the small daily moments that they love and appreciate. Children want to know we care. They need to know they belong, and that we're available.

Although it hurt to hear those words from my daughter, I am proud of her for sharing her truth with me. As a parent, I have some work to do, but I wholeheartly believe we can repair and build a new foundation based on truth and love. I hope my daughter can understand and accept that I did my best, and that I love her so much. I pray that god will lighten her heart and take away her pain. Maybe then she can see my love for her.

S. ABDULLAH

Because I Love You

This gift is dedicated to the ones I love, in the present, and the ones I will not meet in this life. May this gift create love and understanding. Any good I spread, may it be accepted, and any fault overlooked and forgiven.

Prelude-Past lives: *Duality is part of life, in this world let it be healing.*

When we met, I felt important. We played card games together, I could feel the cool hardness of the natural wood pressing against the skin of my little five-year-old legs. The sun was shining in through the drapes of our Seattle home. I remember your beautiful smile as we laughed. To me, those times mattered. I mattered then. As a child, I believed and trusted that would last. I saw myself through your eyes, and I wanted to be your interpretation of who I was. I wanted to please you. I wanted to matter.

There was a time I saw beauty shining back at me in your eyes, and then that reflection changed. The reflection became a projection of your pain and your suffering. And so over time, I become that too. In time, your pain moved past reflection and manifested as violence. Hurtful actions. Words of suffering and the absence of connection.

You passed on your suffering, memories of your childhood cruelties, and your tragic unmet needs. With each blow, our ancestor's pain imprinted into my fragile body. Like a gifted burden. I wanted to matter, so I held your pain for us. I held their pain for us.

Your pain became my pain and pushed through my young body. You taught me fear, shame, and abandonment as they taught it to you. Your suffering embedded itself into my memories, and every cell of my body. Pulsating through my body, it erupted into fists that fought in dimly lit high school hallways. Our pain purged from my mouth like daggers, cutting innocent hearts. It became the haunting whispering companion with a reminder of shame and inferiority.

I loved my college years. I was grown. This is where I blossomed, losing myself in deep thinking and learning. When we met, I felt important. Our intellectually simulated conversations lasted for hours. Together we explored the small shops that lined the back streets beyond the college campus. I felt joy as we walked together from class to class, day-after-day. Happiness surrounded my heart, seeing you after calculus waiting in the fluorescent glow of the white hall. Your face filled with a smile. You offered me a cup of hot chai tea to soothe my sore throat. Our wedding was full of faces smiling with joy and hope. There was happiness. Us together was belonging.

Part I: the Stirring: *Knowing my natural disposition, I am me.*

Over time the gentle touches and joyous connection were replaced with harshness and rejection. The turmoil between us reopened suffering I unconsciously held. I felt triggered by each fallout. I felt exposed. I felt shame. I lost myself in the interpretation of me. Believing that my nature was the cause. Accepting I was not enough to be loved gently.

The looping tape playing in my head continued to remind. Assessing my every action. Do better— give more, work harder— repeat. No matter how many repeats I attempted, the interpretation of me was all you recognized. It eclipsed me. I was not seen. I was not heard. I held our pain and dissolved into believing I wasn't enough.

I stayed because I believed in love— in us— in Allah. I became tired of holding on. To be enough, I let go. Each time I made Salat-ul-Istakhira, the guidance was to stay. The last time I made Salat-ul-Istakhira, in the sunlight of that Saturday afternoon, the unfolding began. When the heart speaks, it can't be ignored. It takes a lot to muffle the wisdom sent encouraging movement. I let go because I believed in love. In me. In Allah.

Part II: The Unfolding: *There are parallel truths even when there are lies, but how others see us is not how we define our self.*

It was toward the end of our marriage that all the brokenness showed itself. It flooded me, pulled me, and pushed me. The ravaging pain of a broken heart. The disappointment of broken dreams. Witness that I wasn't the only victim. My hurting was hurting others. I felt panic. I felt shame. I felt regret.

Violence is an action, and so is healing. So, I lost myself in learning again. I attended Islamic studies classes and lectures. I sought to learn the skills I didn't have—to identify my feelings. I freed the feelings that were locked away for so many years. I learned to see my needs. I learned to ask for help. I learned to listen and communicate.

I took self-improvement classes, read books, and attended healing workshops. I set aside reflection and self-care time, and love showed up. Love showed in the sunrise. In the coolness of the water on a hot day. In the beauty of a bird song. This love was all around me and part of the human experience.

The acceptance I longed for and searched for in the eyes of others, I felt in the most unexpected space. The space of the front door shutting behind me as I walked away knowing the divorce was final. It was in that small infinite space that I found love. A love that had been with me always. I could not recognize the unfamiliar gentleness.

Part III: The Becoming: *Life is meant to be shared, and the best place to start is with oneself.*

In my healing, I can no longer hold the pain. When whispering memories of cutting words, hurtful hands, and lost innocence resurfaces, I refuse to run; instead, I nurture my brokenness. I ground myself in reminders of my spiritual relationship with my Lord. The reminders I placed around my home pull me back from the deep.

The Shahada hanging above the hallway leading into the kitchen reminds me of my purpose. Cascading vibrant green potted plants and glittering crystal rocks remind me of gratefulness and blessings. My care plan written on the bathroom mirror reminds me that healing is a continual action. Dhikring with deep inhales of sage, and Palo Santo brings peace.

Prayer in the late nights and early mornings, grant relief. I find fulfillment. I feel safe. I feel love.

    I let it go, our pain…my pain. I forgive you, myself, and the ancestors who left the pain behind. I found a purpose from the pain. To heal. I feel peace. I am grateful to show up as the best version of myself each moment of each day. In showing up as my best self, I offer space for others to do the same. This is my purpose. I feel compassion. This is my human experience. I can pass on pain or peace. I chose to pass on the gift of love.

LARNETTE SLADE

Lessons to Blessings

At a young age, my parents told me, "What goes on in our house, stays in our house." I grew up holding a lot of my feelings inside. I was never taught how to deal with uncomfortable emotions. I had to deal with my unhappy thoughts alone. I didn't open up and share. It was like I didn't develop good self-esteem until I was in my forties. Sometimes people see me as challenging and outspoken. It feels good to share my thoughts and feelings. Now, I feel confident, like a queen. It was the only way I could grow. I needed to release what is on my mind and not worry about what others thought. If I hurt their feelings, it's too bad.

Growing up, I had a family member who bullied me. She walked all over me. I was put down allot. It seemed every time I said something, my thoughts were shot down. I was never good enough. I have since learned to speak up for myself. I know my voice matters, and I'm not afraid to use it.

At times I feel this new change has shocked a few people. I see myself on the defensive end because of the way I was treated as a child. I always seem to have my guards up when speaking to a certain family member. To this day, this person raises their voice and talks down to me. To help with this, sometimes I pray before I text or call difficult family members.

It's very hard to trust my family with my problems. When I share my issues, they often talk behind my back. Some have said that I have no control over my son. They brag that my son has been in and out of the corrections system since he was fourteen-years-old. I know that to be true, but why gossip about me to strangers?

I heard negative talk about my past relationships, some were true, but didn't understand why they spoke so dirty about me. I rather they say the person is no good, rather than smile in our face, and talk behind our backs. The way I see it is no one has room to talk. Everyone needs to look in the mirror before they talk about anyone else.

My son began staying out all night at the age of fourteen. Every time I would hear on the news that an African American male got shot, was involved in a crime, or killed, I would think it was my son. I constantly took time from work to attend his court cases. I was in and out of the court rooms, meeting with lawyers, and school principals. As time passed, he spent time in multiple correctional facilities. I chose not to discuss my problems with anyone. I was never taught to deal with difficult situations.

In school, we were told to draw a picture of what we wanted in life. The common theme was a big house with a white picket fence, mom, dad, kids, and maybe a car, and pet. Everything on that sheet of paper looked happy. No one told me about disappointments, divorce, hurt, and pain. No one told me that my family would treat me like I didn't matter.

I was never taught that it's okay to talk about how I felt. I believed I had to carry a façade when engaging with others. Often, I would respond, "I'm good," but deep down inside, I was having major issues. I didn't want everyone in my business, but by hiding my pain, I wasn't standing in my truth.

I feel society wants you to experience pain by yourself, without showing any emotion. Self-care was always an after fact. No one discussed prevention. I believe there is power in teaching young people how to deal with their emotions in real time.

As I've matured, I realize I haven't always been put in the healthiest relationships. When I was growing up, our father had a live-in handyman who lived in our basement. He would walk my sister and me to and from school each day. He was like a father figure to us.

We would stop by the corner store after school on 19th and Union for chick-o-sticks, sour balls, and other types of candy. One day, I remember in the back room of our family house, Mr. Smith asked my sister and me to put on our sheer matching pastel gown, and robe set. One was pink, and the other one was yellow.

He asked my sister and me to lay on the bed. He told us not to say anything to anybody. He promised when we got older, he would buy us each a brand-new car. As we laid on the bed, he climbed atop our little bodies and began humping us. I was eight at the time. Thank God, there was no penetration.

He smiled in my parent's faces every day, knowing he was molesting their daughters. My sister and I never told our parents or anyone about this terrible chapter in our lives. It may be because we trusted Mr. Smith, and we didn't know any better. If I had to do it all over again, I would've told my parents. I'm certain had my father found out he would've killed him.

My Father didn't play when it came to his girls and his family.

At this point in my life, I can't even bring it up to my mother. Due to her age and declining health, I'm unsure how she would process it. My mother put up with a lot of things when we were younger. My sister and I asked our mother when we were teenagers why she put up with our father's abusive ways. Our mother's response was," I didn't want you to grow up without a father."

As I reflect on the experiences I witnessed as a child, I can honestly say my mother is a very strong and beautiful lady. She has no filter. She says what is on her mind. I asked my mother a while back if she knew of any family members who were molested. She responded, "Yes, but we never spoke about it."

I believe our family's inability to address the actions of others, has contributed to my attachment to bad relationships. Many of the men I've dated have been alcoholics or drug addicts. They would start out being caring and well mannered, then they would show their true self over time.

My life became whole when my son was born. It was April 12th, 1993, the Monday after Easter. The sun was shining bright, and the flowers were getting ready to bloom. It was a very special day for our family, especially my son's father. He was happy our son was born. DaRaine is a very special child. We love him, dearly. His nickname as a child was Pay-Pay. DaRaine's father named him Pay-Pay because DaRaine loved money.

DaRaine lived with me and my daughter Brittany, or Lady Bug as we affectionately called her. My niece Shaleese name her Lady Bug at a young age, and still calls her that to this day. Brittany is a very smart young lady. She was able to beat the odds. She graduated from high school in June of 2008, and my grandson, Davion, was born that July. Brittany attended her senior year pregnant. She moved out of my house when my grandson was four months old and hasn't lived there since. Brittany has always worked. She was never on public assistance. She is very independent. I'm very proud of her.

I was a single mother, and I worked hard to take care of my kids. DaRaine would go with his father on weekends, and when he came back home, it would take three to four days for him to act right. DaRaine's father didn't teach him to respect me. He would say bad things about me. We didn't work as a team to raise him as a successful young man. If I could do things over again, I would, and it would be different.

When DaRaine was fourteen-years-old, he attended Washington Middle School. He started getting in trouble less than two weeks after his 1st year of 6th grade. DaRaine got into a fight at the local Walgreen's Pharmacy after school. Since he was a student of Washington Middle School, he was suspended for two weeks, even though it didn't happen on the school's property. The School District was criticized a year later for suspending African American students excessively.

I have worried about my son for the last eleven years. He has been in and out of the court system for many years. A positive outcome is he was blessed to have a beautiful daughter.

♛

In 2018, DaRaine was released from the Washington State Department of Corrections to attend a parenting program. The program allows eligible inmates to participate and reside in the community under electronic monitoring surveillance. This was a chance for DaRaine to spend quality time with his daughter, Daveah. Shortly after his entry into the program, my son had a violation.

A few days later, we were together, eating pizza and hot wings when we heard a knock on the door. The hard was hard and intentional. When we opened the door, officers from the Department of Corrections (DOC) were waiting. My son was arrested and taken back in custody in front of us.

DaRaine was broken, he wanted to cry badly. We were told earlier that week that his violation would be reviewed by a hearing officer. We were lied to and betrayed. Even though my son violated his probation, DOC was very sneaky in how it was handled.

This last experience has been a wakeup a call for our family and DaRaine.

DaRaine is grown, I had to realize that his decisions are his choice. He is aware of what is right and what is wrong. My son's incarceration has affected my mind, body, and soul. I hope and pray that he gets his life together for his young family. DaRaine will hopefully come home from the Department of Corrections in May of 2019. I pray this is his last go around with the court system.

My son's time in prison was a wakeup call for me. I was brought up not to discuss what goes on in my house; however, my silence kept me trapped in my body. I didn't build boundaries with men. I wasn't sure what was normal or abnormal. All I know was I was blessed to have both of my parents in our home. I did my best to love, protect, and support my children.

Now, I'm able to talk about my experiences and not be ashamed of the past. I really want to grow and become a better, healthier person. Thank you, Brown Girls Write for allowing me to share my story. The bar has been raised. I'm ready to live, be happy, laugh, and take care of myself. I've found the new beautiful me.

TRINA BAKER

Survival of the Fittest

Crash-boom! I awaken to the impact of a crushing metal and being flipped upside down. The music played loudly as the car tumbled and then became still. *Am I dead?* It's 2:00 am after a night at the club. The last thing I remember was being a few blocks away, trying to stay awake at a red light. I reminisced on a conversation I had a few moments prior, "Are you going to be ok to drive?" my friend asked. "I'm good," I reassured her. My house was just a few miles away, but I struggled to stay alert. I sat up straight, clenched the steering wheel, then turned up the music in an attempt to wake up.

Life was good. I was at the height of my teenage years. At eighteen, I was legally an adult. I was a senior in high school, working for my dad's business—making great money, which allowed me to live on my own. Months before, I fell into a low-key rebellious phase where I resorted to teenage antics, but I always had boundaries, morals, and values that kept me grounded.

In that phase, I was caught shoplifting. My heart pumped as the mall security guard called my mom. I will never forget the feeling of my heart beating out of my chest. I feared jail or death by the hands of my mother. She had to leave work to come and get me over a pair of overalls that I had the money to buy.

Following the stealing episode, I was on restriction, but I was within days from turning eighteen. I dismissed all the rules and gave my mother a parenting adios. I had no rules, an eyebrow piercing, and enjoyed fancy dinners at the Space Needle with my heartthrob boyfriend. I felt ready to conquer adulthood.

I was the youngest, making my mother an official empty nester. Of course, karma works in mysterious ways; it has a way of circling back. It's true what comes around goes around. As a result of my stunts, my eyebrow piercing got infected and pushed itself from my body, permanently scarring my perfect brow. To make matters worse, my high school sweetheart became the first traumatic relationship of my young adult life.

It's interesting being a pastor's kid. There's a solid foundation that you are accustomed to abiding. The day of the accident was no different. One of the conditions of having the car was a commitment to attend church service. My father was a pastor and businessman. Each Friday, I popped into his church for service, then collected my allowance. Hours later, my friends and I were preparing to party the night away. This was the reality of being family-oriented and helping to manage my father's business, while maintaining an active social life.

The car accident was my first encounter with death. It was the first of four accidents that I've since miraculously survived. This night, my mother was abruptly awakened in the middle of the night by police informing her of the accident. I was unharmed but crossed four lanes and hit a telephone pole. I'm positive she'll always remember this call. It came a few months after the rebellion phase, which ultimately humbled our relationship. I couldn't drive because of my injuries, so my mother stepped in to ensure I graduated high school.

I remember cleaning out the totaled vehicle with my father, and he found a bottle of liquor. He was grateful it wasn't found at the scene. I was thankful I was not drunk at the time of the accident. We adjusted from the loss and moved onward, fully acknowledging the spiritual covering over my life.

During this same period, I was desperately in love. My sweetheart insisted a long-distance relationship wouldn't survive college. I allowed his advice to steer my life. Our relationship turned into a five-year heart pumping roller coaster, of love and hate. Somewhere in the middle, we welcomed our daughter.

The baton of motherhood was handed to me at nineteen-years-old. When I delivered my daughter, she came into this world without a manual, just a lot of on-the-job training from my mother. I thought life after turning eighteen was the pinnacle of living, becoming pregnant wasn't a part of the plan.

My mother's existence is very similar to my current life, single living on the out skirts of the city while striving to maintain stability for my daughter. She frequently hears, "Go to college, live in the dorm, join the sorority, and meet your husband on campus." All these things I've said jokingly, but the truth is, it was my dream before I started acting grown. I've asked my parents, 'Why didn't you make me go to college?" My mom laughs in disbelief each time I utter those words. In retrospect, I wouldn't have listened if she tried.

At thirty-seven, I dread the thought of completing college while working a full-time job. Attempting to juggle school seems like a mountain too high to climb, so instead, I push my seed to the top of the peak—hoping she'll fly high once she leaves the nest. Her graduation is an homage to those of us who didn't have the opportunity to attend college. There is power in knowing she can change the trajectory of her life and leave a legacy for the daughter she will not meet.

Like the legendary Maya Angelou said, "Still I rise." The knowledge of family history contributes to the development of self-identity. Our bloodline is thick in Native American heritage. I stand in the footsteps of wisdom warriors holding everlasting hope and strength for our family. In them, there are buried secrets, uncovered tactics, victories, and deep-rooted spiritual hymns. In our ancestors, I see me. In my daughter, I see my younger self.

Raising my beautiful baby girl feels like deja vu. On my path of motherhood, I've learned to take on the role of, "survive don't tell," an inherited trait passed down as a byproduct of mental dysfunction. I recall our mother being divorced with three kids making moves that I didn't realize. Our reality was sheltered.

During this transition, my parents went through the motions of co-parenting. I experienced an unbreakable bond with both parents unaware that they struggled to co-exist. My parent's protection led to spoiling, which attributed to my carefree, and wild lifestyle.

As my daughter approaches the cornerstone of my experiences, I feel the time is of the essence. While the past has taught tough love, I now have the endurance, strength, courage, and wisdom to break generational cycles. As we grow, we constantly pull from the root, dropping new seeds mixed with decades of connected experiences. As I continue to teach my daughter, I will learn from my mother, and the mothers I've never met.

Timeless Tales,

Trina Louise, daughter of Trudi Louise, daughter of Thursa Louise, daughter of Effie St. Claire.

ABOUT THE AUTHORS

Memoirs of a Broken Queen is published in partnership with Brown Girls Write—a self-care initiative aimed at helping women of color reflect, heal, and thrive through expressive writing. Join us on our mission to help 100,000 women of color heal at www.browngirlswrite.org.

Made in the USA
Lexington, KY
30 October 2019